Five Months on the Missouri River

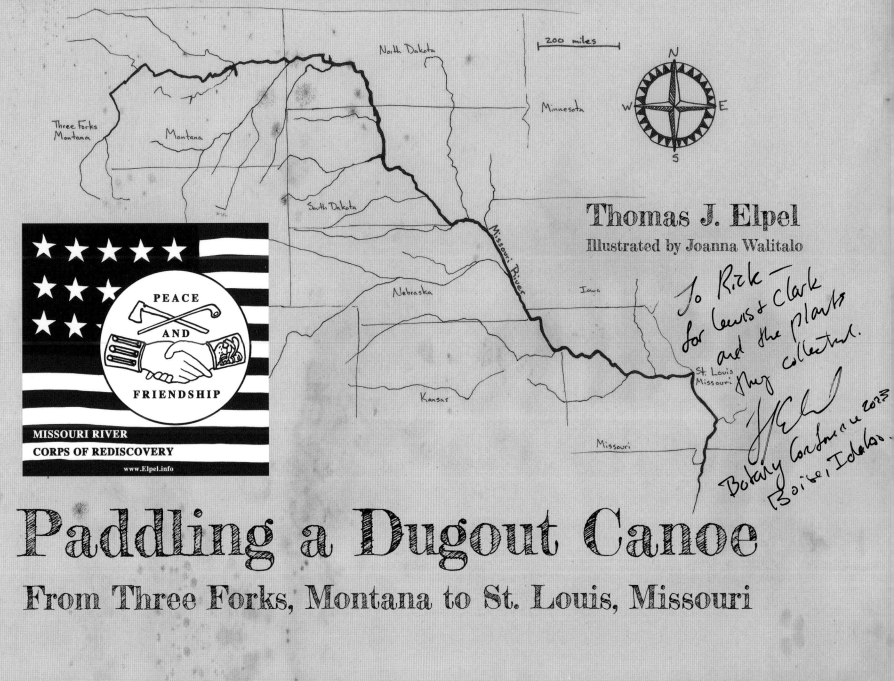

200 miles

North Dakota

Minnesota

Three Forks
Montana

Montana

South Dakota

Missouri River

Thomas J. Elpel

Illustrated by Joanna Walitalo

Nebraska

Iowa

St. Louis
Missouri

Kansas

Missouri

To Rick —
for Lewis & Clark
and the plants
St. Louis they collected.
Missouri
J. Elpel
Botany Conference 2023
Boise, Idaho.

PEACE
AND
FRIENDSHIP

MISSOURI RIVER
CORPS OF REDISCOVERY
www.Elpel.info

Paddling a Dugout Canoe
From Three Forks, Montana to St. Louis, Missouri

MW00668693

Five Months on the Missouri River
Paddling a Dugout Canoe
From Three Forks, Montana to St. Louis Missouri

© March 2020
Thomas J. Elpel
HOPS Press, LLC
Pony, Montana
www.HOPSPress.com

Publisher's Cataloging-in-Publication Data
Elpel, Thomas J. 1967-

Five Months on the Missouri River /
By (Author) Thomas J. Elpel, (Illustrator) Joanna Walitalo

ISBN: 978-1-892784-50-6 $30.00 Pbk. (alk. paper)

1. Missouri River—Discovery and Exploration
2. Missouri River—Description and Travel
3. Canoes and Canoeing—Missouri River
4. Missouri River—Pictoral Works
5. Lewis and Clark Expedition (1804-1806)—Guidebooks
6. Lewis and Clark National Historic Trail—Guidebooks

I. Elpel, Thomas J. II. Title.

F592.7.E47 2020   917.8042 ELPEL 2020

Table of Contents

"We are now several hundred miles within the bosom of this wild and mountanous country, where game may rationally be expected shortly to become scarce and subsistence precarious without any information with rispect to the country not knowing how far these mountains continue, or wher to direct our course to pass them to advantage or intersept a navigable branch of the Columbia, or even were we on such an one the probability is that we should not find any timber within these mountains large enough for canoes if we judge from the portion of them through which we have passed."

—Meriwether Lewis at the Missouri Headwaters, July 27, 1805

The big log arrives!

Genesis of a Dream

Every wilderness expedition is a spiritual journey. Being exposed to the elements entails an implicit vulnerability, whether backpacking, horseback riding, or canoeing. Embracing the raw wild is an opportunity to leave behind the comforts and security of home, to cast oneself into the hands of the Universe on a journey of faith that everything will be alright.

We set up shop at River camp.

Even the best laid plans entail a degree of risk. Stormy weather can blow trees or tree limbs down on a tent. Lightning can strike on land or water. Sudden winds can blow so hard it is near impossible to paddle to shore, and big waves can swamp a canoe in the middle of a lake. I've talked to other Missouri River paddlers who experienced tornado-like conditions, in one case seeking shelter in a concrete restroom for protection while their tent was destroyed by the wind. There is no guarantee of safety.

I've learned to trust that the Universe will carry me through when I walk the right path. That being said, I am not a risk-taker nor an adrenaline junkie. My brain doesn't process information fast enough to handle whitewater rivers or downhill skiing. I gravitate to slow sports like backpacking, cross-country skiing, or paddling Class I rivers with no significant rapids. Other people can revel in the thrill of the wind whipping past their faces while sky-diving or bungie jumping. I'll revel in the thrill of finding and photographing wildflowers I've never before seen.

Flattening the bottom with a chainsaw.

Genesis of a Dream

Most of my walkabouts and canoe trips last a week or two, but as a recent empty-nester, I sought a greater adventure. Three possibilities tantalized my imagination: hiking the Appalachian Trail, bicycling across the United States, or paddling the length of the Missouri River from Three Forks, Montana to St. Louis, Missouri. The Universe decided for me through serendipitous intervention.

I originally envisioned paddling the Missouri River in a modern canoe, but suddenly had the opportunity to fulfill a longtime dream to carve a dugout canoe when I connected with Churchill Clark, the great-great-great-great grandson of Captain William Clark of the Lewis and Clark Expedition. He retraced the Lewis and Clark journey from St. Louis to the Pacific Ocean and back in a dugout canoe during the 2004 to 2006 bicentennial. He now travels the country "carving canoes and paddling trees."

Chopping off the pieces.

Chruchill knocks a block loose after we roughed out the inside with a chainsaw.

I forgot about it until now, but my interest in paddling a hollow log likely started with a log ride at an amusement park decades ago. The fast and scary rides didn't interest me much, but the log ride resonated on some deeper level. Sit and take a slow ride up, tick-tick-tick-tick, then crest the top and slide down the watery chute to the big splash at the bottom. It's interesting how life swirls in currents, bringing forgotten childhood moments to life decades later.

Thanks to Meriwether Lewis and William Clark, the hollow log is the archetypical adventure story of Montana. The Corps of Discovery began their ascent of the lower Missouri River in 1804 with a big keelboat and two smaller boats known as pirogues, over-wintering in present-day North Dakota. In the spring of 1805 they sent the keelboat back downstream and later abandoned the wooden pirogues in favor of hand-carved dugout canoes for the shallow waters of the upper Missouri.

The principal object of their mission was to ascend the Missouri in search of a navigable water route with an easy portage over the Rocky Mountains and down the Columbia River to the Pacific Ocean. On July 27, 1805, they reached the confluence of three rivers that merge together to form the Missouri River not far from my home in southwestern Montana. Lewis and Clark named these tributaries the Jefferson, Madison, and Gallatin rivers after the President, Secretary of State, and Treasury Secretary. They proceeded up the Jefferson River before hiding the canoes and acquiring horses from the Shoshone Indians to cross the Rocky Mountains. In 1806 the Corps of Discovery retraced their path back to St. Louis, exploring side routes along the way.

My first time in the canoe!

My family history mingles with the Missouri Headwaters. Grandparents Orville and Josephine Jewett farmed near the Jefferson River, living for a time in a two-room log cabin with a sod roof. Originally known as the Parker Homestead, the cabin remains in the family, still visible along U.S. Highway 287 near the town of Willow Creek. My mother wrote the original John Colter pageant in 1958, which was enacted at the Three Forks rodeo grounds, kicking off the town's first Colter's Run.

Generations of involvement and interdependence at the Headwaters cemented my dream to carve a dugout canoe, a dream that weaved seamlessly with my life-long interest in wilderness survival skills and bushcraft.

As the founding president of the Jefferson River Chapter of the Lewis and Clark Trail Heritage Foundation, an organization for the purpose of securing a water trail with campsites along the 80 mile Jefferson River, it seemed only natural to paddle a dugout canoe.

Fifteen years ago I hired a neighbor to cut and haul a cottonwood log "big enough to carve a canoe," but the tree provided was only one-fourth the necessary diameter. As Meriwether Lewis observed, large cottonwoods are scarce here above the Missouri Headwaters where the larger plains cottonwood (*Populus deltoides*) gives way to the skinnier narrowleaf cottonwood (*P. angustifolia*). The log was repurposed for campfire benches.

The bottom lines are quickly taking shape.

Genesis of a Dream

Trimming the sides with a Log Wizard.

Connecting with Churchill re-ignited the dream, so I invited him to Montana to work together on a dugout canoe. The timing was fortuitous. His last project consumed one-and-a-half years to carve two dugout canoes from a tall cottonwood tree in Missouri. We planned to work on the new canoe together the following spring and hopefully cut the timeline down to two or three months.

About the same time, my friend Steve Morehouse donated his retired dugout canoe as a museum piece for River Camp, a field camp for my business Outdoor Wilderness Living School LLC (OWLS) where I teach survival skills to public school kids. In addition to the canoe, Steve offered to sell me the canoe trailer he had custom built for the big canoe. I doubt there are many dugout canoe trailers in existence, yet this one serendipitously came to me when needed.

Following an intuitive path isn't always easy or logical. I found another tree that seemed large enough for the dugout canoe, so Churchill came to Montana to oversee the project. However, as he pointed out, there wouldn't be much left after removing the bark and the softer sapwood to make a nice canoe. Therefore, anything less than 36 inches in diameter is too small for a good canoe, and my tree was just barely too small.

In a pinch and panic, we called around in search of a big enough tree. I ultimately bought a massive old Douglas fir from a sawmill. Douglas fir is not a traditional canoe wood, because it is hard and full of knots and it cracks and pops like popcorn as it dries, but we believed it would work. The knots necessitated extensive use of power tools to aid the traditional adze work.

Churchill saw a beaver face in the bow and started carving it into the design.

Local school groups came to River Camp to learn about the canoe carving process.

It took nearly three months of sawing, chopping, grinding, and sanding–plus a good bit of epoxy, linseed oil, and varnish–to turn the 10,000-pound log into a 500+ pound canoe.

Early in the process, Churchill observed the image of a beaver face in the bow of the canoe and started carving it into the design. I had merely envisioned a functional canoe, but he created a work of art, which is so beautiful that I ultimately named her Belladonna Beaver. The end product is far more beautiful than a cottonwood canoe.

Nevertheless, I remained skeptical ahead of our first test run. We drove 260 miles with 'Bella' in tow to spend a week paddling the Marias River in north-central Montana. On arrival, it didn't seem like there was enough water to float the boat, but Churchill assured me it would work, and he was right, the test run was a fantastic success.

Almost finished.

As Churchill noted, a cottonwood loses half its weight as it dries, while a Douglas fir loses only ten percent. It is a very heavy canoe. Nevertheless, Belladonna Beaver floated beautifully and paddled like a dream. We enjoyed a week exploring the Marias River as a good test run to prepare for the Missouri Expedition the following year. I started planning the adventure immediately after we returned home.

My goal for leading a "Missouri River Corps of Rediscovery" was to paddle the river as a conduit for exploring the land and meeting its inhabitants, rather than to merely race for the finish line. Living on the river for the extended adventure offered a great opportunity for botanizing, foraging, and fishing as we explored the geographical landscape and met the indigenous and newly integrated flora, fauna, and human habitations.

First time in the water!

We enjoyed a week-long test run down the Marias River.

I floated the expedition proposal though social media to invite friends, former students from my Green University® LLC program, and strangers to join me for five to six months to paddle the 2,341-mile river from its beginning near Three Forks, Montana to its end, where the Missouri joins the Mississippi at St. Louis.

Few people were able to walk away from their jobs, families, or other commitments to join the adventure, but I was lucky to find a few good men to accompany me on the journey: Scott Robinson, John Gentry, Chris Dawkins, and Josiah Fischer, the latter three having been prior students at my Green University® LLC program. I've lived around the Missouri Headwaters most of my life. It was time to take a leap of faith and see where all that water goes!

See Belladonna Beaver on YouTube:
Look for *Dugout Canoe Carving: The Story of Belladonna Beaver*
and *Dugout Canoe Paddling: The Marias River Adventure*
Subscribe to https://www.youtube.com/user/thomasjelpel for more canoe adventure videos.

I envisioned a simple dugout canoe, but gained a work of art, which I named Belladonna Beaver.

Montana

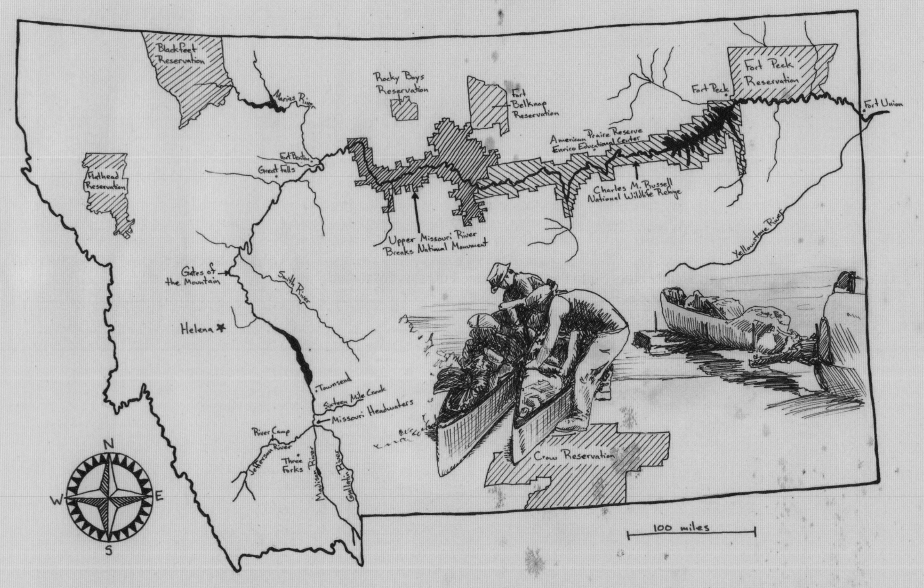

Blackfeet Reservation

Marias River

Rocky Boys Reservation

Fort Belknap Reservation

Fort Peck

Fort Peck Reservation

Fort Union

Flathead Reservation

Fort Benton

Great Falls

American Prairie Reserve
Enrico Educational Center

Charles M. Russell
National Wildlife Refuge

Upper Missouri River
Breaks National Monument

Yellowstone River

Gates of
the Mountain

Smith River

Helena

Townsend

Sixteen Mile Creek

Missouri Headwaters

River Camp

Jefferson River

Three Forks

Madison River

Gallatin River

Crow Reservation

N
W E
S

100 miles

"This little fleet altho' not quite so rispectable as those of Columbus or Capt. Cook were still viewed by us with as much pleasure as those deservedly famed adventurers ever beheld theirs; and I dare say with quite as much anxiety for their safety and preservation. we were now about to penetrate a country at least two thousand miles in width... and these little vessells contained every article by which we were to expect to subsist or defend ourselves. however as this the state of mind in which we are, generally gives the colouring to events, when the immagination is suffered to wander into futurity, the picture which now presented itself to me was a most pleasing one."

--Meriwether Lewis departing the Mandans, April 7, 1805

The Journey Begins

Preparing to launch off the trailer.

Our little fleet consisted of two modern canoes plus my dugout canoe, and five men to pilot them down the river—not so respectable as Columbus, Capt. Cook, or Lewis and Clark, but still viewed by us with equal pleasure as we embarked on our own journey of discovery.

We launched from Missouri Headwaters State Park near Three Forks, Montana on June 1st to begin our five-month voyage downriver to St. Louis. Friends and well-wishers came to see us off, and seven other paddlers joined us for the day in their own canoes and kayaks.

Sunny skies and warm temperatures invited us onto the water. After a long, lingering winter in the northern Rockies, we felt fortunate and grateful that summer arrived at all. Lewis and Clark must have felt similarly after overwintering with the Mandan Indians in present-day North Dakota in 1804-1805 through brutally cold temperatures and the relentless winds of the Great Plains.

Calculating from latitude and longitude, the explorers estimated a journey of at least two thousand miles from the Mandan villages up the Missouri River, over the Rockies, and down the Columbia River to the Pacific Ocean. Our journey was far less ambitious, and we flowed with the current, not against it, yet we still faced a

Josiah Fischer, John Gentry, Scott Robinson, Chris Dawkins, and Tom Elpel.

13

Several other paddlers also joined us for the day.

My friend Ken Younger came for the send-off and paddled with us.

Ready to launch!

Limestone cliffs of the 1,700-foot thick Madison Group formed from 359 to 326 million-year-old carbonate deposits on the seafloor.

journey of more than two thousand miles winding down the sinuous Missouri River to St. Louis.

We enjoyed a leisurely first day, drifting ten miles with the current to camp at Fairweather Fishing Access Site. In the spirit of Lewis and Clark, we dined on bison burger, chopped and fried with dandelions, wild mustards, and plantain leaves. Norm Miller, organizer of the Missouri River Paddlers Group on Facebook, dropped in for a nice visit to wish us well on our journey. Norm paddled UP the Missouri in 2004 as part of the Lewis and Clark Bicentennial.

Bison burger and wild greens.

Photo by Norm Miller

Missouri River paddler Norm Miller visited our camp.

15

With dry weather and not yet many mosquitos, we opted to forgo tents for the night, each of us sleeping under different juniper trees for shelter from the morning dew. For breakfast we collected plantain leaves and mixed them in a batter of flour, egg, water, and spices, then fried them in butter in the wok over the campfire.

The river called us onward, and we drifted downstream through the scenic canyon to Sixteen Mile Creek, which Lewis and Clark originally named Howard's Creek after Thomas P. Howard, a member of the expedition. We were joined by Adam, who launched two weeks earlier, paddling down the Beaverhead and Jefferson rivers to join us on the Missouri for a while. We all stopped under the railroad bridge to explore the ruins of the historic town of Lombard as long freight trains rumbled back and forth down the line.

If Lewis and Clark were alive today, they would easily recognize the river they explored, but they might not believe it. In four months dragging their dugout canoes upstream through present-day Montana, they did not encounter another

We all slept under juniper trees.

human being until they were near present-day Idaho. Montana remains one of the least-densely populated states, yet there are more than a million people here now, largely crowded along river corridors. The Missouri is lined with trains, highways, cities, towns, and coffee shops, plus ten dams just in the Montana portion of the river.

Toston Dam was our first obstacle on the Missouri, only 30 miles from our launch. No worries. With a boat ramp, trailer, and volunteers to shuttle us around the dam, portaging would be nearly effortless, or so we anticipated... before learning that the boat ramp was temporarily closed.

We were fortunate to enjoy lovely weather after a chilly, wet spring.

Watching the train roll by at Lombard.

Ratcheting Belladonna Beaver across the grass.

We never weighed Belladonna Beaver the dugout canoe, but optimistically claimed that it weighed 500 lbs. In actuality, four men cannot lift the front end of the canoe, so the total weight might be closer to 1,000 lbs.

By weighting down the back, lifting the front, and winching from a tree, we succeeded in getting her head out of the water and on the grass. Switching to the next tree, we pulled Belladonna across the grass on PVC pipes as rollers, then towed her forward with a rope from the truck and ultimately used a car jack to get her head high enough to load onto the canoe trailer.

We used a jack to raise the canoe to the trailer.

The few hours required to complete the portage was nothing compared to what Lewis and Clark endured portaging upstream around the Great Falls of the Missouri, yet we were proud of our accomplishment and felt a degree of kinship with their challenge and experience. It was empowering to know we could overcome obstacles and portage the canoe if we had to. We only hoped we would never have to do it again!

Loaded and ready to go.

17

"Saw a great abundance of the common thistles; also a number of wild onions of which we collected a further supply. there is a species of garlic also which grows on the high lands with a flat leaf now green and in blue but is strong tough and disagreeable. found some seed of the wild flax ripe which I preserved; this plant grows in great abundance in these bottoms. I halted rather early for dinner today than usual in order to dry some articles which had gotten wet in several of the canoes."

—Meriwether Lewis, July 23, 1805

Tall buttercup (Ranunculus acris).

Botanizing the River

President Thomas Jefferson tasked Meriwether Lewis with more than merely following the Missouri River to its source to seek a potential water route to the Pacific. Jefferson commanded Lewis to study the geography and geology of the route, to note any useful resources, and to document the plants, animals, and fossils encountered along the way.

Herein is the enduring appeal of the Corps of Discovery. Rather than blindly race to the end, they engaged in a scientific journey of discovery, collecting samples and journaling about their observations. Lewis recorded the above observations near Townsend, Montana, on their ascent of the headwaters, very near one of our campsites.

In a similar vein as Lewis and Clark, our five-month "rediscovery" of the Missouri River was more about exploring the river than merely paddling to the end. Time along the river offered an opportunity to identify new plants, forage for wild

Morning rainbow.

First carp taken with the fishing bow!

foods, hunt carp with bows and arrows, learn new birds, and seek to better understand bird language. The end goal of paddling to St. Louis provided a convenient excuse to spend five months camping, hiking, and exploring, slowly changing scenery as we migrated downstream. Otherwise, if the objective were merely to get to St. Louis, I would have driven there.

The need to overcome nature, to climb a mountain or paddle a river, is built into our culture, embedded in our history of conquest and colonization. It is symptomatic of a fundamental disconnect. Plants are green and birds sing songs. We don't know the plants and animals in our neighborhood; we are largely blind to species we encounter every day.

We yearn to connect with nature, and not knowing how to do that, we treat nature as an adversary more than a dance partner. We pit human endurance against nature and seek to overcome her. We bask in the glory of our accomplishment while missing nearly everything along the way.

Fried carp with morel mushrooms and watercress greens.

Bald eagle nest and family.

Lewis and Clark were the very face of conquest and colonization, yet they also sought to learn about and understand the land and its inhabitants. Lewis recorded many previously unknown species of plants and animals, made detailed observations about them, and inquired into the customs of native peoples along their route. In two and a half years, the expedition cumulatively wrote more than a million words in their journals, providing readers today an opportunity to experience the journey through their eyes. From an ecological perspective, the journals are invaluable for comparing present species composition with observations noted by Lewis and Clark two hundred years ago.

As a botanist and author of *Botany in a Day* and *Foraging the Mountain West*, every outing becomes a botanical adventure, an opportunity to discover new plants and potential new wild foods. We enjoyed great salads of dandelions, plantain leaves, watercress, and wild mustards. It was fun hunting for morel mushrooms and common carp. This upper stretch of the Missouri River is close to my home and a regular haunt for hunting both.

Common carp (*Cyprinus carpio*) were originally native to Europe and Asia and fish-farmed for centuries. In some countries carp is still considered a Christmas delicacy. Carp were introduced to North America as a food source, becoming widespread and highly invasive, ultimately disdained by Americans as bottom feeders and trash fish. Few people eat them, but I've found them delicious, fatty, and crazy abundant.

We scored a nice bunch of morel mushrooms at York's Islands near Townsend. Scott found his first-ever morel, followed by many more.

Carp spawn when water temperatures reach 60°F in the spring. They swarm up from the depths of Canyon Ferry Lake to spawn in shallow reeds along the lakeshore as well as in backwater sloughs off the river.

The Montana Bowhunter's Association sponsors a "Carp Safari" every June where fisherman boat across the lake and spend the day hunting carp. Individuals and teams compete for the biggest carp or the most carp caught, measuring and weighing them before tossing them all in a construction-sized dumpster. Some years they nearly fill the dumpster with carp, which makes no measurable difference in the carp population in the lake. MBA seeks cooperative farmers with land to compost the massive pile of fish.

On July 24, 1805, Lewis noted "a remarkable bluff of a crimson coloured earth."

We host our own carp safari, sometimes spending a week paddling the river while we hunt, fillet, cook, and feast on carp. Fried carp with barbecue sauce is amazing. Batter-fried carp is the best. We've even packed a pressure canner along to can jars of carp for winter, used much like tuna fish. Detailed instructions for filleting and processing carp are included in *Foraging the Mountain West*.

Paddling the western shore of the river, we passed by the "crimson bluffs" noted by Meriwether Lewis. The bluffs are composed of 1,400-million-year-old Greyson Shale. Sergeant Patrick Gass recorded that Sacagawea spoke of using the red earth for paint. The site was in danger of being developed for housing until the Crimson Bluffs Chapter of the Lewis and Clark Trail Heritage Foundation secured conservation funding to purchase the fifty-acre property, passing it along to the Bureau of Land Management to maintain it for public use.

Charging batteries with the solar panel.

We continued downstream to a favorite campsite on a riverfront parcel of state land with a carp-filled slough, which I call Crimson Bluff Slough. Although we paddled only five miles for the day, it was a great place to stop and take a layover to hunt carp, hike, explore the desert hills, and take time for bird watching.

Cooking carp and bison heart.

John took a turn with the fishing bow.

Jim Emanuel stopped by. He paddled from Three Forks to the Gulf of Mexico in 2018.

Nice catch John!

The slough was thick with carp when we paddled in. John borrowed the fishing bow and caught several for dinner. We filleted the fish and cooked batter-fried carp for breakfast.

Wild food foraging includes an element of experimentation, and I've been eager to play with grass pollen, or rather the whole stamens stripped off of grass flowers. A Timothy-like grass grew abundantly in the damp meadow, so I gently stripped the stamens off with my fingers. Pollen is highly nutritious, and I imagine the stamens are too. I mixed them with equal parts wheat flour and some water to make "ashcake dough," so-called because the flat biscuits are cooked directly on the hot coals. The end product tasted more-or-less like any other ashcake, but presumably more nutritious.

After playing my *Shanleya's Quest Patterns in Plants Card Game* at our previous camp, we enjoyed a hike up through the desert hills identifying the plant families we encountered. My crew mates were learning botany and foraging from me, yet I was not the only one teaching. Each person had something to share, and the group was constantly practicing skills, making bow and drill fire sets out of different woods, twining cordage from yucca fibers and wild licorice stalks, sharing bushcraft philosophy and carving techniques. Each day brought a new and exciting journey.

Batter-fried carp for breakfast.

The "how to" manual.

I collected grass stamens as flour.

We enjoyed morel mushrooms and bison burger for dinner.

"The country was rough mountainous & much as that of yesterday untill towards evening when the river entered a beautifull and extensive plain country of about 10 or 12 miles wide which extended upwards further that the eye could reach   this valley is bounded by two nearly parallel ranges of high mountains which have their summits partially covered with snow.   below the snowey region pine succeeds and reaches down their sides in some parts to the plain but much the greater portion of their surfaces is uncovered with timber and expose either a barren sterile soil covered with dry parched grass or black and rugged rocks."

—Meriwether Lewis, July 21, 1805

Wind Faeries

Meriwether Lewis noted the sudden transition from rugged or "mountainous" canyon to open valley. This transition point would become the site of Canyon Ferry Dam, built by the U.S. Bureau of Reclamation 150 years later as part of the Pick-Sloan Plan authorized by the Flood Control Act of 1944 and completed in 1954. The dam is 225 feet tall and 1,000 feet long, a fairly small cork to make a reservoir 1 to 3 miles wide and 30 miles long. The name Canyon Ferry was retained from gold rush days when a ferry operation helped transport prospectors across the river.

While Lewis and Clark entered the valley dragging or poling canoes upstream against the current, we paddled downstream with the river. Where they found a wide, shallow river filled with islands, we found a big lake ruled by a malevolent Wind Faeries.

Paddling the river itself is easy, mostly drifting with the current and steering as necessary. Paddling the length of a big lake is altogether another matter. There are now fifteen dams on the main stem of the Missouri River, forming 700 miles of artificial lake. We were enjoying a pleasant day until we reached Canyon Ferry Lake and the wind suddenly kicked up, lifting big waves with it.

Paddling into choppy waters on Canyon Ferry Lake.

We landed on the beach, only to swamp Belladonna with waves.

We should have heeded the advice of other paddlers to follow the western shore since the wind usually blows from that side across the lake, but I was hoping to visit points along the east side. Maybe it wouldn't have mattered, since the wind this day blew directly out of the north-northwest. However, the east side features a series of artificial duck ponds rimmed with steep banks of rocky rip-rap, rendering it impossible to land in stormy weather.

We paddled furiously into the headwind, parallel to the bank, going nowhere fast. I don't know how many hours it took to clear the four-mile length of the duck ponds, but Chris and I took the first sandy beach we encountered, hoping to land Belladonna and drag her by leash along the shore. That only made a bad situation worse.

The waves hit the stationary canoe and rolled right over the sides, swamping her in seconds. We bailed furiously, hopelessly trying to empty the canoe faster than she filled, when all of a sudden the Wind Faeries vanished, leaving us with a beached whale and opportunity to assess our situation.

We picked willow catkins as an experimental food.

Three of our four canoes were partially or wholly swamped. We bailed water, repacked, and were blessed with a gentle tailwind to push us along at 3 mph using handheld kayak sails. Upon finally reaching camp, we did as Lewis and Clark did, taking time to *"dry some articles which had gotten wet in several of the canoes."*

On the river we could paddle through variable weather, but exposed on the lake, we were forced to layover and wait for wind and weather to pass. We stayed at Confederate Campground, our tents wholly protected from the wind behind a thick belt of willows.

Being windbound the next day, we seized the opportunity for additional botany and foraging. I was curious about willow catkins, the staminate or male flowers, which taste mildly sweet. We harvested a pile of them, which looked suspiciously like mealworms, then added them to a dough of flour and water to make fry bread. Like the grass flowers, the willows didn't add much flavor, but probably added good nutrition. For dinner we cooked up a mess of nettle greens to compliment our Polish sausages and willow catkin fry bread.

Willow catkin - wheat flour cakes.

While we enjoyed our sheltered camp, Belladonna Beaver remained moored at the water's edge and by morning she was full of water like a bathtub. I borrowed a bucket from our campground neighbors to bail her out.

I learned critical lessons from the Wind Faeries: Never land the canoe on a beach perpendicular to the waves, and never camp on the lakeshore without a suitable harbor to protect my ship.

However, the big problem remained: Paddling the lake isn't particularly fun with a headwind, or even a tailwind, or no wind at all. Moreover, the heavy, blunt dugout canoe moved notably slower than the lighter, sleeker modern canoes. I knew we would eventually make it across Canyon Ferry Lake. It was the vastly bigger lakes downstream that worried me.

The crew indulged me in exploring the feasibility of linking our canoes together in series to paddle as a unit down the reservoir, which minimally helped. My other big idea was to try hitch-hiking across all the lakes with a towrope behind anyone we could flag down with a motorboat. It seemed like a good idea.

Jim Emanuel returned with his motorboat at my request. It didn't seem practical to hook multiple canoes to the motorboat for the test, so the guys generously allowed me to link up and speed across the lake without them. As captain of the expedition, I think that was an especially poor judgement call, abandoning my crew like that.

Incoming waves filled Belladonna Beaver like a bathtub during the night.

We experimented with towing the dugout behind Jim Emanuel's motorboat.

The Wind Faeries apparently disapproved as well, blowing a fierce wind out of nowhere while Chris and I hung on for dear life behind the motorboat. I stuck my paddle out behind, desperately trying to rudder Belladonna to keep her properly aligned, fearing any second we would be completely swamped by the waves. The experience was as exhilarating as it was terrifying. After what seemed like three or four miles, I finally yelled for Jim to stop and let us go. Chris was already wet and chilled from water coming over the bow, and he leapt up onto Jim's boat when he stopped to unite the knot. I paddled to shore. Jim came as close as he safely could with the propellor, leaving Chris to wade to shore half-hypothermic.

Handheld kayak sails and a gentle breeze helped move us across Canyon Ferry.

The Wind Faeries once again disappeared as quickly as they came. Looking back, we'd only come one-third of a mile and the rest of the crew hadn't even launched due to the big wind. I started a fire to warm Chris while everyone else paddled to catch up, and we camped right there.

The Universe works in mysterious ways, especially on wilderness adventures. The Wind Faeries seemed to admonish me for abandoning my crew. I wouldn't do it again.

The next day we paddled to Hellgate Campground, a few miles shy of Canyon Ferry Dam, but close enough. My Uncle Joe and Aunt Diane brought my trailer to portage us around the dam. Scott's girlfriend Margie brought a cousin with another trailer to help with the other canoes. It was good to be off the lake.

Canyon Ferry Dam as seen from Riverside Campground.

Passing under York Road bridge.

Silverweed cinquefoil (Argentina anserina, formerly known as Potentilla anserina)

We paddled the length of Hauser Lake in one day.

Aunt Diane (and Uncle Joe) helped us portage.

"This evening we entered much the most remarkable clifts we have yet seen. These clifts rise from the waters edge on either side perpendicularly to the height of [about] 1200 feet. every object here wears a dark and gloomy aspect. the tow[er]ing and projecting rocks in many places seem ready to tumble on us. the river seems to have forced it's way through this immence body of solid rock for the distance of 5 3/4 miles and where it makes it's exit below has thrown on either side vast collumns of rock mountains high. the river appears to have woarn a passage just the width of it's channel or 150 yards... from the singular appeaerance of this place I called it the gates of the rocky mountains."

—Meriwether Lewis, July 19, 1805

Bitterroot blooms opening (Lewisia rediviva).

Gates of the Prairie

The Gates of the Mountains are celebrated among the most iconic, scenic highlights of the Missouri River, yet Meriwether Lewis mysteriously found them "dark and gloomy." I pondered his words as our expedition of rediscovery paddled into the canyon. Lewis previously gave high praise to the White Cliffs. What triggered his disdain for the Gates? Was it due to practical concerns or a reflection of his propensity for melancholy?

I imagined the Corps of Discovery working upstream against the current in the twilight hours more than a year into their ascent of the Missouri River since they left St. Louis. Their recent portage around the Great Falls turned into three weeks of unimaginably brutal labor. Above the falls, the Corps assembled Lewis's custom-designed iron frame boat and consumed precious time covering it with skins, but lacked any pitch to seal the seams. It was a spectacular failure. On the heels of these setbacks, the Gates must have seemed ominous indeed.

We awoke to a gorgeous morning to paddle into Gates of the Mountains.

Unlike the White Cliffs area, where the river was slow and the banks wide, the narrow Gates made it impossible to walk the shoreline with ropes to drag heavy dugout canoes upstream. Nor could the men use poles to push themselves forward against the bottom. Their only recourse being to paddle furiously against the swift current, consuming precious energy to merely avoid floating backwards.

Add to that the unknown, and the uncertainty of what lay around the next bend. By any reasonable expectation, the river could have been filled with great boulders that sloughed off the canyon walls to create impassible rapids or yet more waterfalls. With the expedition ascending the canyon in the twilight hours and no place to halt and camp, it is easy to imagine the towering cliffs, shadowy holes, and streaked rock faces as dark and gloomy.

The Gates were quite the opposite for our little expedition. We were feeling worn and beaten after the arduous paddle across the artificial lakes at Canyon Ferry and Hauser dams. My personal gear was in disarray and not wholly dry after twice swamping the dugout canoe with waves on the shores of Canyon Ferry. My Uncle Joe and Aunt Diane graciously assisted us with the portages around each dam, delivering us exhausted yet renewed to the Gates of the Mountains. We camped at the mouth of the canyon, drinking in the beauty of the landscape.

My sister Jeanne joined us the following day. We shuffled gear and seating arrangements to

My sister Jeanne joined us to paddle through Gates of the Mountains.

*Tom Muenster (second from left) led the
Upper Missouri River Expedition by pontoon boat.*

bring her onboard and marveled at the fantastic cliffs and bonsai juniper and ponderosa pine trees growing from the rocks.

Funny how the rugged, wild landscape Lewis disdained is now what we treasure. Seven generations after his passing, we have carved up nearly every arable piece of land for roads and farms and cities, leaving only the most inhospitable scraps of wilderness in their pristine state. So precious is this wasteland of rocky cliffs that tour boats ply the river daily as tourists throng to see a remnant of the untouched world.

In the canyon we met up with Tom Muenster of South Dakota, who was leading a two-week Upper Missouri River Expedition by pontoon boat in honor of Sergeant Patrick Gass of the Corps of Discovery. The five veterans were touring sections of the river between Three Forks, Montana and Sioux City, Iowa. We exchanged trade goods in the middle of the lake.

Glover's silkmoth (Hyalophora gloveri).

The land is regenerating after a 2007 fire.

I greatly enjoyed hiking with my sister!

Moonlight in the canyon.

31

John leads the way on a forest trail as we climb up out of the canyon.

The swift river Lewis ascended through the canyon is no more. Holter Dam backs water up fourteen feet deep through the canyon, and motor boats speed back and forth covering in minutes what took us two days of paddling.

Our expedition encamped at Coulter Campground for two nights, named for John Coulter (or Colter) of the Expedition. It was a wholly appropriate place to read a passage from Stephen Gough's book *Colter's Run*, a great work of historical fiction based on Colter's life.

Our layover day provided the opportunity to hike the trails, to study new flowers together, and to learn new birds. Chipping sparrows and western tanagers accompanied us on our walk. Bald eagles were everywhere along the water.

Arrowleaf balsamroot (Balsamorhiza sagittata) lights up mountain meadows.

We stayed two nights at Coulter Campground.

Like Lewis and Clark, we dined well. We were largely prepared to live off dry staple foods this trip, yet have daily enjoyed gourmet meals. Adam contributed the bison burger and bison heart. Scott's girlfriend Margie baked elk meatloaf and brought it to camp. We did our own batter-fried carp fillets and enjoyed trout and walleye caught by Scott. My aunt and uncle treated us to cheeseburgers and fried chicken at portage points. Friends and well-wishers gifted us beef pasties and chocolate chip cookies. Here we savored Canada goose gifted to us frozen a few days prior by fellow paddler Jim Emanuel. With rhubarb imported from my mother's garden, I baked a pie for dessert. It felt like glamping more than camping!

Looking downriver from the Meriwether Picnic Site.

We enjoyed a final glimpse of canyon splendor before paddling beyond Gates of the Mountains.

Although the lake bustled with motorboats, we had the campground largely to ourselves. Most people apparently prefer to consume nature for lunch and return home with ample time for dinner and a sitcom. But one gal we met had it figured out. She motored out on the lake to camp in the evening, then commuted to work from there each day. She and her friends joined us for a pleasant evening around the campfire before retiring to the boat to sleep.

We could have easily stayed longer ourselves, but destiny called us onward. Paddling out in the morning, we stopped to view Indian pictographs on the canyon walls. Paddling the length of Holter Lake through the winding canyon, the cliff

Indian pictographs can still be seen on the canyon walls.

*Paddling towards
Bear Tooth Mountain.*

*Blanket flower
(Gaillardia aristata).*

walls gradually transition to grassy hills. The skyline remained dominated by jagged peaks, but no longer the snow-capped mountains of home.

Ponderosa pines, absent in the upper reaches of the Missouri, now dotted the hills where soil moisture permits, creating open, grassy forests. This is the same species that grows to immense height and girth in moister climates, and from which Lewis and Clark carved canoes in present-day Idaho for the descent of the Columbia. These prairie ponderosas were comparative dwarfs and bound to get smaller the farther we traveled east into prairie country.

John found the remains of an elk apparently killed by a mountain lion in the Beartooth Wildlife Management Area, the carcass abandoned to a scavenging bear that turned tail and disappeared upon his approach. The WMA is closed to camping, so we stayed on the opposite shore.

Scott caught a walleye in the lake.

Montana / June 14 / Holter Lake / Beartooth Wildlife Management Area to Holter Dam

Here we met Mark Juras, who was paddling from Three Forks to the Gulf of Mexico in a rowboat/kayak of his own creation. With the aid of mirrors mounted on the boat, he could see behind him to row backwards the entire 3,600-mile journey.

Continuing our journey of rediscovery, the Gates of the Mountains became our Gates of the Prairie as we followed the route of Lewis and Clark in reverse. We were blessed with a tailwind to deploy the sails for the final stretch of Holter Lake. My mother met us with the truck and trailer to portage the dam, and Jeanne relinquished her seat in the canoe. Another camp, another night, and the adventure continued, now back to free-flowing river.

Lake Holter was as still as glass in the morning, giving a perfect reflection.

Wild rose (Rosa woodsii).

We took a rest stop to explore the small fishing town of Craig, Montana.

Nice trout!

John and I made a salad of cattail shoots, prickly lettuce, and sprouted lentils.

37

*Dalmatian toadflax
(Linaria dalmatica)*

"At this palce there is a large rock of 400 feet high wich stands immediately in the gap which the missouri makes on it's passage from the mountains; it is insulated from the neighbouring mountains by a handsome little plain which surrounds its base on 3 sides and the Missouri washes it's base on the other, leaving it on the Lard. as it decends. this rock I call the tower. It may be ascended with some difficulty nearly to its summit, and from it there is a most pleasing view of the country we are now about to leave. from it I saw this evening immence herds of buffaloe in the plains below."

—Meriwether Lewis, July 16, 1805

Ghosts of the Tower

For Meriwether Lewis, Tower Rock was the beginning of the transitional zone from open prairie to the Rocky Mountains looming beyond. Coming from the opposite direction, the river meanders through a fairytale land of purplish-brownish rock hills, knobs, and cliffs of the 75-million-year-old Adel Mountains Volcanic Field, of which Tower Rock marks the downstream end. We were privileged to experience this scenic and enchanting float while the volcanic formations were accented by brilliant green spring vegetation.

Looking down towards camp at Spite Hill Fishing Access Site.

*Lunch break in the Adel Mountains Volcanic Field
a few miles before Tower Rock.*

The river wound back and forth under Interstate 15 through the volcanic field, emerging at Pine Island Rapids, the only significant rapids on the entire Missouri River. We paddled around the worst of the whitewater, tied up our canoes at Hardy Creek, and followed the small stream up to Tower Rock State Park.

Climbing the tower served as a stimulating diversion for a bunch of river rats, an opportunity to look down upon the world instead of up. To the West is a great view of the volcanic fields, to the East is the open prairie, and down below is the hustle bustle of the interstate, with cars, trucks, and semi-trucks careening down the road, drivers jockeying for position to take the lead and win the rat race to nowhere.

Above the ceaseless roar of the highway is another sound, deafening in it's silence, haunting in its absence, the ghosts of Lewis's "immence herds of buffaloe" that no longer thunder across the plains. It is difficult to fathom so much change in so little time.

Passing under the Interstate 15 bridge.

Lewis observed "immence herds of buffaloe" from this vantage point at Tower Rock.

Scarlet globe mallow (Sphaeralcea coccinea)

History creeps ever closer as we age. Lewis and Clark seemed unfathomably ancient when I was ten years old, seventeen lifetimes ago to this child of the 1970s. The passage of time should push history that much farther into the past, yet the opposite is true. At age 51, only four lifetimes now separate my journey from theirs.

Photo by Scott Robinson

Botanizing at Tower Rock State Park

It took slightly more than one of my lifetimes to exterminate the buffalo and subdue the Indians, another to homestead and build settlements and railroads. In the third we built the great dams, cities, and highways, and in the fourth, our time, we gobbled up the resources of the earth in an orgy of consumerism, with bigger houses, bigger toys, and bigger bellies.

Beyond the Tower we paddled into true prairie country with rolling grassy hills and broken, calving riverbanks. Massive plains cottonwood trees, big willows, and shrubby box elder

White pelicans (Pelecanus erythrorhynchos) are common along the Missouri River throughout the summer season.

trees lined the way. We stopped in Cascade for lunch, then on to Little Muddy Creek to camp. Chris foraged a salad of plantain leaves, topped with bright yellow silverweed cinquefoil flowers for garnish. Adam cooked spaghetti squash and meat sauce for our first course, followed by two rainbow trout caught by John and Scott. We haven't lacked for good food!

Morning reflections.

A beautiful sunny day on the river.

Plantain leaves garnished with yellow flowers of silver cinquefoil made a colorful and tasty wild salad.

Ghosts of bison are everywhere, this one in Cascade.

More trout!

41

Montana / June 18 / Little Muddy Creek to Ulm

We awoke to a beautiful sunny day with perfect reflections on the water. Sometimes we paddled down the river; mostly we just drifted like turtles on a log soaking up sunshine. But we dallied a little too long, getting caught in an afternoon thundershower. Less than a mile ahead, the bridge at Ulm offered protective shelter. Chris and I paddled furiously while the storm pounded us with rain and hail. By the time we reached the bridge, we were soaked, and the storm was over. We camped at the Ulm Fishing Access Site immediately after the bridge. Like many fishing access sites, this one was officially closed to camping. But when the site manager swung by, she could see we were doing no harm, and we lacked any other place to go. In true Montana style, she issued a special use permit consisting of a business card and a handshake.

We awoke to a beautiful sunny day in camp at Little Muddy Creek Fishing Access Site.

These mourning dove chicks were in a nest on the ground.

Time to kick back and soak in some sun.

A storm pounded us with rain and hail just before we reached Ulm.

Raccoon tracks on the beach.

We toured First Peoples Buffalo Jump State Park.

Bison provided shelter, clothing, food, and tools.

The following day we hitched a ride to First People's Buffalo Jump, four miles off the river. The interpretive center museum was first rate, and the ranger's talk was stellar. We learned the intricate methods by which Native Americans coaxed the herd to follow a stray calf, in this case a boy or buffalo runner wearing a robe, who led the herd towards the cliff until they could be stampeded over the edge.

While significant, the number of bison killed at buffalo jumps was minuscule compared to the tens of millions later hunted with guns for their hides or tongues or the mere entertainment of shooting them from windows of tourist trains like mobile video arcades.

Like Tower Rock, First People's Buffalo Jump is rife with ghosts of the past, not so much of bison who fell to their deaths, but rather the ghostly presence of hundreds of millions who never lived. The wind blows a silent tune over the cliffs; there are no buffalo at the Buffalo Jump.

Ghosts of the past are not easily forgotten. They surface when least expected. Three years ago I pulled a nearly perfect buffalo skull from the banks of the Jefferson River. Last year I paddled by two more in the Marias River. Of all the mammals on earth today, only 4% are wild animals, rapidly declining as our population continues to rise. Will we continue this trajectory until there are no more wild things or wild places?

The bald eagle tells us there is hope. Our national emblem, the bald eagle was nearly wiped out by cumulative effects of the pesticide DDT until it was banned in 1972. Bald eagles have since bounced back, and we were pleased to encounter them on nearly every bend of the river, a plethora of adults, juveniles, nests, and nestlings.

The American Bison is equally iconic to our country, and very nearly went extinct. But what would America be without bald eagles or bison? In 2016 Congress designated the American Bison as our national mammal, recognizing its symbolic importance to our national identity. In that designation there is hope.

Like the bald eagle, we can restore the bison, at least where appropriate on wildlife refuges and Indian Reservations. Maybe someday, when another Corps of Rediscovery follows the Lewis and Clark National Historic Trail, they will actually see bison from some of the same vantage points as Meriwether Lewis and William Clark.

A'aninin, Assiniboine, Cree, Kalispel, Piegan Blackfeet, Salish, and Shoshoni tribes all utilized the First Peoples Buffalo Jump.

Montana's most popular paddling destination, the Smith River enters the Missouri below Ulm. I paddled it with my family fourteen years earlier.

Morning sun on the prairie river.

Chris cooked while Josiah entertained.

Wild rose close-up

I seldom photographed houses, but this castle is unique on the riverfront, built by a Great Falls doctor.

"I went with the p[arty] for the remainder of the baggage. we got all and was returning. Saw a black cloud rise in the west which we looked for emediate rain   we made all haste possable but had not got half way when the Shower met us and our hind extletree broke in too   we were obledged to leave the load Standing and ran in great confusion to Camp the hail being So large and the wind So high and violent in the plains, and we being naked we were much bruuzed by the large hail. Some nearly killed   one knocked down three times, and others without hats or any thing about their heads bleading and complained verry much."

—Sergeant John Ordway, June 29, 1805

We toured the Lewis and Clark Interpretive Center.

A Hail of a Portage

Portaging around the Great Falls of the Missouri required eleven days of brutal work for the thirty-one men of the Corps of Discovery in 1805. Following their route in reverse, we did the portage in a day, accomplished as easily as making a phone call.

Lewis and Clark learned of the Great Falls through talks with the Mandan Indians over the winter of 1804-1805 in present-day North Dakota. They were told to expect a half-day portage around the falls, advice from people who traveled the area on horseback, rather than boat.

Instead of a single waterfall, the explorers found five cascades spread out over ten miles. The Corps improvised wooden wheels and axels of cottonwood to convert their dugout canoes into wagons, which they pushed and pulled over steep hills along the river. When they weren't suffering from mosquitoes on the river, they suffered from searing hot weather, crazy storms, and prickly pear cactus spines in their moccasins. The work was so intense that the men were prone to falling asleep standing up when they paused. As if that wasn't enough, they were hit by golfball-sized hail that caused serious injuries.

Their larger wooden pirogues were too big to portage, and thus hidden below the falls. The crew attempted to assemble Lewis's lightweight iron frame boat, but failed for lack of pitch to seal the seams. They ultimately carved two more

The Corps of Discovery dragged heavy canoes miles overland to portage the Great Falls.

47

dugout canoes, consuming a total of thirty-one days at the Great Falls before proceeding up river.

Sharing our story with children.

Nowadays there are fifteen dams on the Missouri River, including five dams at Great Falls. As in 1805, it is still necessary to portage around the entire Great Falls complex in one move, but fortunately, the portage is much easier. Canoeists can call a shuttle service to portage canoes, gear, and people downstream beyond the dams.

Belladonna Beaver, however, is no lightweight canoe. She has her own custom-built dugout canoe trailer, complete with rollers and a winch to reel the canoe in place. We would need the trailer for every portage as well as for the return trip to Montana. I didn't see any choice but to bring the trailer with us.

Ryan Dam at Great Falls.

Migrating a trailer down the river might sound like a logistical nightmare, but it went astonishingly well. Family members helped us portage the first four dams and parked the trailer in Great Falls. My friend Jeff would pick it up there to meet us for the portage around Fort Peck Dam in a few weeks. I didn't do much actual planning; it just fell together as each person indicated when they wanted to visit.

Back at Ulm we hit a short, but intense rainstorm that soaked us before we reached shelter under a bridge. That same storm dropped baseball-sized hail farther north in Valier that totaled vehicles, broke house windows, and heavily damaged siding and roof shingles. Fortunately, we missed that part of the Lewis and Clark experience.

On portage day, we started early and paddled ten miles from our campsite to Broadwater Bay in town, then called Montana River Outfitters to bring the trailer. They outsourced the job to Jim and Phyllis, who gave us the royal treatment in town.

They delivered Belladonna Beaver and I to the Lewis and Clark Interpretive Center for the afternoon, where I talked with visitors and a large class of children about the canoe and our expedition.

Hand-hewn wheels facilitated the overland journey.

Meanwhile, Jim and Phyllis drove the crew around to get lunch, view the falls, and visit a sporting goods store. Everyone had an opportunity to tour the Interpretive Center before we hitched up again and headed out of town.

Afternoon storms raged through while we were in the museum and again later while driving down the highway to Carter Ferry, tapering off before our launch. We unloaded, repacked our gear, and paddled down the river looking for a campsite.

Another rain squall forced us to be less choosy. Near Cherry Coulee we set up tents in the rain and hunkered down for the night. While the landscape above Great Falls is prairie country, the river below cuts through badlands with steep, eroding cliff faces. It is beautiful, harsh, and rugged country, and we were excited for the continuing journey of rediscovery.

"Arduous Journey" sculpture by Carol Grende features Sacagawea and Pomp.

Black Eagle Falls and Dam.

Photo by Scott Robinson

Carter Ferry provides free shuttle service for vehicles across the Missouri River.

Sculpture of Sacagawea, Lewis, and Clark seems to poke fun at the many depictions of the explorers pointing the way.

"I sent out 4 hunters this morning on the opposite side of the river to kill buffaloe; the country being more broken on that side and cut with ravenes they can get within shoot of the buffaloe with more ease and certainty than on this side of the river. my object is if possible while we have now but little to do, to lay a large stock of dryed meat at this end of the portage to subsist the party while engaged in the transportation of our baggage &c, to the end, that they may not be taken from this duty when once commenced in order to surch for the necessary subsistence."

—*Meriwether Lewis, June 20, 1805*

Catching a light breeze on the river.

Tools and Provisions

The Corps of Discovery worked unimaginably hard dragging heavy dugout canoes upstream against the current. They famously ate nine pounds of red meat per person per day, the equivalent of eating thirty-six quarter-pound hamburgers—minus lettuce, pickles, tomatoes, and buns. Feeding the expedition for one day required either four deer, an elk and one deer, or one whole buffalo. Suffice it to say, the members of our Corps of Rediscovery ate somewhat less, and we didn't shoot any deer, elk, or buffalo—not even a grizzly bear.

Photo by Scott Robinson

After Great Falls we dropped below the prairie into rugged badlands.

Perhaps the most under-appreciated accomplishment of the Corps of Discovery was their preparation work. Originally envisioned as an expedition of twelve soldiers with Meriwether Lewis in command, Lewis bucked convention by naming army buddy William Clark as co-captain. The rank was rejected by the War Department, yet Lewis and Clark snubbed authority and maintained the fiction of two equal captains throughout the expedition.

Together they enlisted as many men, boats, guns, supplies, and trade goods as they deemed necessary for a journey of unknown duration into unknown lands. They enlisted boatmen, hunters, cooks, and translators, with most men serving double-duty to dress skins, make clothing, or improvise repairs as necessary without hope of resupply.

Increasing the size of the expedition required more boats and more equipment, yet they calculated the magic numbers of essential men and equipment.

Self-sufficiency was paramount, so their equipment emphasized guns, lead, and gunpowder over actual food rations. They carried dehydrated "portable soup" and other rations for emergencies, but largely depended on hunting for the duration of the 2 1/2-year, 8,000-mile journey. As their clothes wore out or rotted away, they tanned hides and made their own. They also carried extensive trade goods to exchange for food and supplies from native tribes. Although largely destitute by the end, they successfully completed the mission.

Through it all, Meriwether Lewis had a desk for his journals and writing implements and probably spent much of the expedition sitting in a canoe journaling while the men dragged the boats upstream. His copious writings bring the expedition to life even now.

A sponge is essential to mop out the canoe.

Preparations for our Missouri River Corps of Rediscovery were less critical, since we would have the option of resupplying in numerous towns and cities along the way or even receiving packages at post offices.

My primary obsession ahead of the canoe trip was to build a custom desk for the dugout canoe. I had forgotten about Lewis's desk, but as a writer, I always pack books, notebooks, and writing utensils first. My desk had a wood writing surface that could be opened to reveal a built-in solar panel for charging electronics. Inside the desk was a small library of Lewis and Clark books, field guides, note pad, iPad, teaching tools, binoculars, a harmonica, snacks, and trade goods, such as the expedition bandannas we gifted to people along the route.

At twenty-feet, Belladonna Beaver was the biggest canoe in the fleet, so she carried an assortment of group gear, such as a bow saw for cutting firewood and a fishing bow to hunt

Unlike Lewis and Clark, we didn't hunt deer, elk, buffalo, or grizzlies.

My pre-trip obsession was to build a custom writing desk to fit Belladonna Beaver.

A small section of Fort Benton's adobe walls remain.

Reconstruction of Fort Benton began in the 1990s, substituting earth-colored concrete blocks for the original adobe bricks.

Fort Benton originated as a trading post to trade with the Blackfeet.

carp. We used a rusty old gold pan for a fire pan to avoid leaving fire scars where fire pits were absent. Collapsible canvas buckets ensured a supply of water near the fire. We used a wok for cooking. I thrust a shovel in the ground in the middle of camp to facilitate digging cat holes when there were no toilets.

Other essential gear included a big sponge recycled from an old couch cushion for mopping out the canoe, plus a livestock stake that could be driven into the riverbank to tie up the canoe. Chris, my main paddle partner, and I each had a ten-gallon locking barrel for clothing and personal gear, plus I had a barrel for food and a small cooler. He had a dry bag and bucket for food, and we had random food and gear tucked into every remaining space. There were no actual seats in the canoe, but we placed our bedrolls in dry bags and sat on those.

As for food, everyone prepared in their own way. I opened up the kitchen cabinets and shoved every partial bag of rice, lentils, flour, pasta, oatmeal, raisins, snacks, etc. into my barrel and called it a month-long food supply. We barely touched our dry goods in the first three weeks of the trip, but topped off with a resupply of cheese, summer sausage, bagels, yams, sweet potatoes, onions, pasta sauce, and snacks for the upcoming month-long gap between Fort Benton and Fort Peck, 300 miles downriver.

The need for tools and provisions gave rise to Fort Benton in 1846 when the Blackfeet Indians asked American Fur Company agent Alexander Culbertson to relocate the newly constructed Fort Lewis trading post to the north side of the Missouri River. The log buildings, bastions, and walls were dismantled and floated downstream then re-assembled at the new site. Inspired by the adobe walls at Fort Laramie, Culbertson decided to upgrade the fort for better protection against extreme cold and wind, completing the adobe structures by 1860.

Staying at Fort Benton's Canoe Launch Campground, I cooked goldeye fish, gifted to us by the camp host, plus French toast and rhubarb sauce.

Trade good were initially brought upriver by hand-powered mackinaws and keelboats, transitioning to steamboats after 1860. Located below the Great Falls and 3,000 miles from the sea, Fort Benton was the innermost port in the world. The Montana gold rush of 1863 brought a surge of miners, settlers, and merchants with tools and provisions to Fort Benton and overland destinations. Fort Benton remained a busy port for thirty years until railroads outcompeted steamboat travel.

A friendly town bunny.

I've been to Fort Benton before, but without enough free time to adequately explore the historic town, so it was refreshing to stay for three nights.

Stopping in at a coffee shop, I serendipitously bumped into German adventurer Dirk Rohrbach and partner Claudia Axmann, who had just arrived in town. I had met them a year earlier when they came to River Camp to interview Churchill about canoe carving for German Public Radio. Dirk then paddled source-to-

Lewis and Clark Memorial by Sculptor Bob Scriver.

The keelboat Mandan was built for the 1952 movie The Big Sky, based on the book by A.B. Guthrie.

Dirk Rohrbach and Claudia Axmann.

sea from Brower's Spring, the utmost source of the Missouri, 3,800 miles down the Red Rock, Beaverhead, Jefferson, Missouri, and Mississippi rivers to the Gulf of Mexico. Dirk and Claudia were traveling by road, retracing the water route to take additional photos for an upcoming book.

Our own little expedition was soon ready to continue onward. Having passed through the towns of Craig, Cascade, Ulm, Great Falls, and Fort Benton, our day-to-day provisions largely transitioned to burgers, burritos, sub sandwiches, and pizza. We were eager to disappear into the wilderness and return to fishing, foraging, and cooking from our own provisions.

Photo by Scott Robinson

A double rainbow beckoned us to continue the journey, now approaching one of the most scenic stretches of the entire Missouri River.

Upper Missouri Breaks National Monument

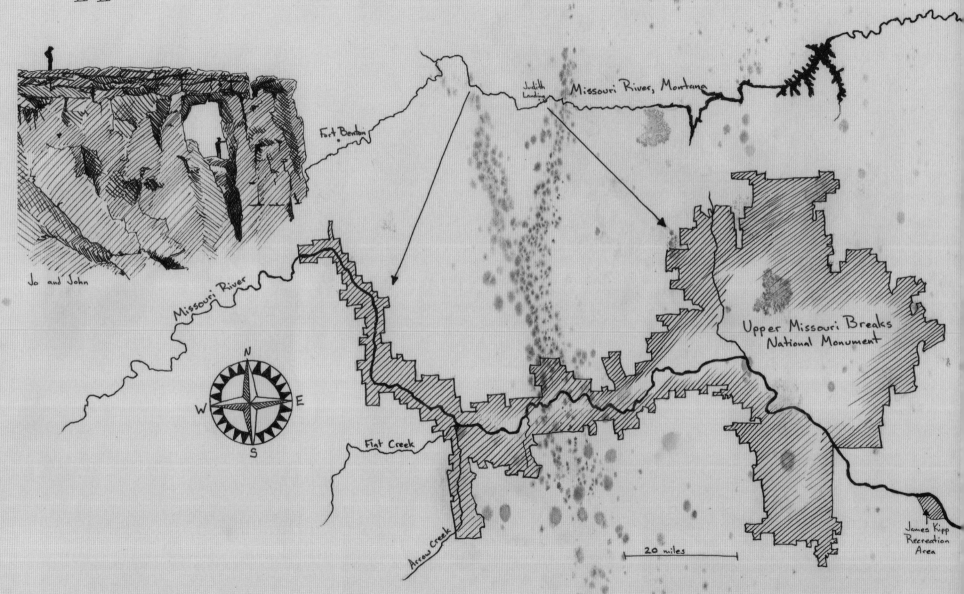

Jo and John

Fort Benton

Judith Landing

Missouri River, Montana

Missouri River

Upper Missouri Breaks
National Monument

Flat Creek

Arrow Creek

N
W E
S

20 miles

James Kipp
Recreation
Area

Scenic badlands near Fort Benton consist of 90-million-year-old grey shale from the Marias River formation overtopped by slightly younger fine-grained sandstone of the Timber Creek Formation, layers deposited when the land was dominated by a vast inland sea.

Scott and Chris paddle the Old Town.

We camped at Senieurs Reach.

Whitetail fawns were common here.

"Today we examined our maps, and compared the information derived as well from them as from the Indians and fully settled in our minds on the propryety of addopting the South fork for the Missouri... [which] I indevoured to impress upon the minds of the party all of whom except Capt. C. being still firm in the belief that the N. Fork was the Missouri and that which we ought to take; they said very cheerfully that they were ready to follow us anywher we thought proper to direct but that they still thought the other was the river and that they were affraid the South fork would soon termineate in the mountains and leave us at a great distance from the Columbia."

—Merwether Lewis, June 9, 1805

American kestrel with prey.

Decisions of Leadership

Fort Benton is neither the official start of the Upper Missouri Breaks National Monument, nor the Upper Missouri National Wild and Scenic River, but the badlands scenery from there on down is equally stellar. We paddled fifteen miles to camp at Senieurs Reach Recreation Area. Here we were greeted by a friendly camping sign at the river's edge and a welcoming plains cottonwood sheltering a fire ring and grill. Senieurs Reach is just a scrap of Bureau of Land Management land perched on the riverbank and surrounded by private land, as yet unfenced and unposted, as was most of Montana in my youth.

A wild turkey guided her chicks to cover.

We watched a pair of kestrels feeding their famished chicks in a hollow branch of the cottonwood. A turkey hen guided her chicks through the snowberry bushes by camp. I nearly stepped on a spotted fawn hiding in the grass. The shrubby box elder trees were full of house wrens, yellow warblers, yellow-breasted chats, and Bullock's orioles. Every time I turned around it seemed I saw another deer or fawn. We saw two bald eagle chicks in a nest perched high up a cliff face. A family of juvenile magpies flocked near me during my morning walk.

Continuing downriver, we paddled to Decision Point, a major fork in the Missouri River and a conundrum for Lewis and Clark. While wintering downriver with the Mandan Indians, the captains questioned their hosts about the upstream course of the Missouri

Evening brought soft colors to the sky over a soft landscape.

River. Through translators aided by maps drawn in the earth, Lewis and Clark learned of the river's significant tributaries and knew to expect the Great Falls of the Missouri. But this fork wasn't on their maps, and it wasn't immediately clear which river was the true Missouri.

John joined me to paddle Belladonna Beaver.

Juvenile magpie.

The south fork was larger and more clear, yet the north fork was substantial and ran muddy brown like the Missouri. Lewis and Clark believed the south fork was the true Missouri, while every other man of the expedition believed they should take the north fork. Choosing the wrong route would likely have ended expedition in failure and probably forced them to overwinter in the mountains where they might starve. Yet, as a testament to Lewis and Clark's leadership skills, the men told them they would cheerfully follow them anywhere.

A bald eagle rests on a fallen tree in the river.

Members of the Corps of Discovery were hand-picked by Lewis and Clark from many applicants. They chose the strongest, most skilled, and experienced men who were also single. Maintaining discipline initially proved challenging among this small army of young, restless men, especially during the winter of 1803-1804, before the official launch of the expedition. Several men were court-martialed and flogged there or after the expedition began. Over time, however, the expedition bonded together towards a common mission.

The Corps of Discovery camped at Decision Point for eleven days to explore both routes before proceeding without a definitive answer, following the co-captains' original intuition. Shortly thereafter, they encountered the Great Falls of the Missouri, confirming the route.

By the time they reached the Pacific Ocean, the expedition achieved a relatively egalitarian level of trust, in which every member of the expedition had an equal right to vote in determining the location of their winter camp, including Sacagawea and Clark's slave York. That was an extraordinary leap forward for democracy, short-lived as it was.

As for the mysterious north fork, Lewis named it Maria's River in honor of a girl he hoped to marry. The apostrophe was dropped over time to make it the Marias River. Churchill and I paddled the Marias River exactly one year ago with other friends, taking Belladonna Beaver out for a week-long test run. As a paddler, it is thrilling to connect one river trip with another, stitching together my own experiential map of Montana.

Wild rose.

Selecting a crew to join me for the Missouri River Corps of Rediscovery required a non-military approach. Flogging a crew member would not be tolerated by them, me, or the law.

I invited friends, family members, former students, and complete strangers via social networks. I trusted the Universe to send an interesting and hopefully compatible crew, one where we could learn from each other's company. Many people expressed interest in the expedition, which self-sorted down to the core group as individuals opted out due to other commitments, health or financial reasons, or otherwise determined it wasn't their time.

Dinner with orache leaves.

My leadership style was necessarily tribal. Tribal chiefs lacked rule of law or mechanisms of enforcement, necessitating leadership that was reasonable, flexible, and persuasive rather than militaristic to keep young bucks in line. That's how it works with young people at Green University®, LLC, men and women follow their own passions and don't care much for rules or authority. It's like herding cats as they explore their own unique interests.

By our launch date of June 1st, the expedition included myself and four other quiet, introverted guys, all with varying levels of experience. Like William Clark, Scott was slightly older than me and our chief navigator, effectively co-captain of the expedition. Where Clark recorded bearings and distances to draw detailed maps of the river, Scott followed digital maps and GPS waypoints to guide us to our chosen campsites.

Invasive leafy spurge blooms yellow on Boggs Island.

John brought a résumé of wilderness survival training more extensive than my own and a passion for exploring the world and

59

We stopped at Virgelle Ferry and walked half a mile to the "town," consisting of one antique store.

Showy milkweed (Asclepias speciosa)

connecting on a deep, spiritual level. Chris was a veteran of many long-distance adventures by foot, bicycle, and hitch-hiking, who brought a particular love of tracking and bird language. Josiah came on as a highly adaptable greenhorn, having sold everything he owned to buy a solo canoe. He received verbal paddling instructions on the banks of the Missouri moments before we launched. We were also joined part-time by Adam, who planned his own expedition, but drifted in and out of our group as we migrated down the river.

We improvised camp on Boggs Island in one of the few spaces free of deep grass and poison ivy, settling in just before a big storm blew through. Josiah bravely finished cooking dinner under a tarp, and we enjoyed eating and talking there until it seemed that even the tarp would blow away. We collapsed it for the night and ran for our individual tents.

The next day brought us by Virgelle Ferry and Coal Banks Landing to Little Sandy Creek Campground, where we slogged through fifty feet of mud to camp. Prior to the Pleistocene Ice Age, the Missouri River flowed north from here around the Bear Paw Mountains to merge with the Milk River, ultimately terminating in Canada's Hudson Bay. Early ice sheets shoved the Missouri south, rerouting it to the Gulf of Mexico. However, the Milk River segment remained open until about 15,000 years ago, when advancing ice forced the Missouri to carve a new channel south of the Bear Paws. Older sections of the Missouri River valley are wide and rounded, but the newly cut channel remains steep and eroded, giving rise to the scenic badlands topography.

Greater short-horned lizard (Phrynosoma hernandesi)

Although one should avoid camping under cottonwood trees in wind and lightning, there was little choice at Little Sandy, but wow, that storm was spectacular! Other paddlers later said the storm packed 70 mph winds.

"The hills and river Clifts which we passed today exhibit a most romantic appearance... The water in the course of time in descending from those hills and plains on either side of the river has trickled down the soft sand clifts and woarn it into a thousand grotesque figures, which with the help of a little immagination and an oblique view at a distance, are made to represent eligant ranges of lofty freestone buildings, having their parapets well stocked with statuary; collumns of various sculpture both grooved and plain, are also seen supporting long galleries in front of those buildings... As we passed on it seemed as if those scenes of visionary inchantment would never have and end; for here it is too that nature presents to the view of the traveler vast ranges of walls of tolerable workmanship, so perfect indeed are those walls that I should have thought that nature had attempted here to rival the human art of masonry had I not recollected that she had first begun her work."

—Meriwether Lewis, May 31, 1805

*Plains clubtail dragonfly
(Gomphus externus)*

Visionary Inchantment

Meriwether Lewis's White Cliffs of "visionary inchantment" mark the start of today's Upper Missouri National Wild and Scenic River, now included within the Upper Missouri Breaks National Monument. This wild and scenic river is remote and accessible primarily to those willing to paddle and camp.

Many people return to paddle this stretch of the Missouri every year. Thus campsites are sometimes full, requiring parties to push on and look for other sites. In comparison to the rest of the world, however, the wild and scenic river is anything but crowded. At peak season, one may expect to see half a dozen groups float by in the course of a day, varying from a canoe

We paddled to Little Sandy Creek, which was more muddy than sandy.

*Spinystar cactus
(Coryphantha vivipara)*

or two up to eight or more. This is my second trip through the wild and scenic corridor, having first paddled it nineteen years ago with my family of five from Coal Banks to James Kipp Recreation Area.

We stayed at the Little Sandy Creek Campground during that trip and this one, then paddled downstream to Eagle Creek.

It was floater friendly campsites like these that inspired my own work on the Jefferson River Canoe Trail. Working with like-minded folks, we identified, scoped, and named isolated parcels of BLM land along the Jefferson, published maps, and have since purchased additional campsites to fill in the gaps. Our most recent acquisition was the 30-acre Lost Tomahawk, named by local school kids after an incident recorded in the Lewis and Clark journals.

Lunch break at Eagle Creek Campground.

At Eagle Creek, Josiah cooked hamburger and made burritos for lunch. We hiked up the creek to view the Indian horse petroglyphs on the cliff face, made by Crow and Blackfoot raiders during the mid-1800s. I would have loved to stay at Eagle Creek for a night or two, but destiny called us onward, so we paddled downstream past Citadel Rock to Hole-in-the-Wall Campground. A large group of paddlers claimed the site ahead of us as

Josiah paddles the White Cliffs area.

We hiked up Eagle Creek, here looking out from the Indian petroglyphs.

Mud at Eagle Creek.

Paddling towards Citadel Rock.

We camped at Hole-in-the-Wall, the actual hole being visible in the cliff beyond camp.

Exploring the sandstone wonderland.

part of a fundraising canoe trip for the Montana Wilderness Association. We moved downstream a half mile to a primitive camp by a lone cottonwood. That was perfect for us, and even closer to the actual hole-in-the-wall, which could be seen in the cliff above camp.

Although the hole is in the side of a cliff, the backside is accessible by foot. Like every hike, this one turned into a botany walk as we encountered new flowers. I found an obvious pea flower like a milkvetch, but with deeply segmented seedpods indicating a sweetvetch instead. Feral orache is abundant on the Missouri. A relative of spinach, the plant became the preferred green to compliment our meals.

The soil remained moist from near daily rain showers. Damp clay slipped underfoot or stuck to our shoes, but was largely avoidable by seeking pathways through the eroding sandstone layers. These mud or shale and

Beautiful country. Josiah pauses for a look back.

Northern sweetvetch
(*Hedysarum boreale*)

sandstone layers formed from 70 to 90 million years ago with the advance and retreat of the inland sea that covered much of North America. Rivers contributed sediments that separated into coarse, sandy particles near shore, with fine clay particles settling in deeper waters to form shale. Uplift and subsidence raised and lowered the underlying land, moving the shoreline back and forth to create distinct layers. Dinosaurs roamed the tree-lined shores.

Sedimentary layers are tilted highest towards the uplifted Rocky Mountains, bringing the 90-million-year-old greyish-blue (black when wet) Marias River shale to the surface upstream of Fort Benton. Paddling downstream takes canoeists forward in time through 20 million years of geologic history.

Most of the layers consist of shale, the source of so much mud. The clay particles swell when wet, making an impervious cap that sheds additional water. The more porous sandstone layers are easily visible from a distance by the evergreen trees, ponderosa pines and Douglas fir, that take root in the more accommodating soil.

We camped at Slaughter River Campground, a short distance upstream from the actual river, so-named by Lewis and Clark after they encountered the rotting remains of bison herded over a buffalo jump by the Indians. Lewis and Clark camped here too, on May 29, 1805, as noted by a bronze marker.

Stiff-stem flax
(*Linum rigidum*)

Paddling towards Slaughter River Campground. A bronze plaque marks Lewis and Clark's campsite a short distance upstream.

Morning sunshine lights up sandstone across the river from Slaughter River Campground.

Harvesting prickly pear pads.

Burning off the spines

Every four or five days we took a layover day, enjoying additional time for bird-watching, botanizing, sewing projects, writing, reading, and relaxing. John caught and later released a gopher snake, also known as a bull snake.

A family of juvenile American kestrels perched on a high branch in a cottonwood tree. Lacking a proper zoom for my camera, I started shooting pictures through binoculars, bracing the contraption on my knee for stability.

Prickly pear cacti were plump with moisture from recent rains. I gathered a nice mess for dinner and torched the spines off on the grill, then scraped them clean and sliced the toasted pads, called nopales in Mexico, before frying them with orache leaves and hamburger for dinner. The cactus provided a slightly slimy but good, okra-like texture to our meal.

We added prickly pear nopales and orache leaves to hamburger for dinner.

Juvenile American kestrels.

John caught a gopher snake.

Floating downriver. Common blue flax (Linum usitatissimum). Squirrel tracks. Woodhouse's Toad (Anaxyrus woodhousii). Sunset at Judith.

Evening sunshine lights up the PN Missouri Bridge, as seen from Judith Landing Campground.

A thick layer of Claggett Shale was deposited by the expanding inland sea overtop the Eagle Creek Sandstone, identifiable by the trees.

Happy camper. Paddling downstream towards towering badlands. John kicks back on a break. Dinner and fry bread. Mountain cicada.

A protected coulee harbors young cottonwoods near McGarry Bar.

"One of the Party Saw a verry large bear, picked up on the Shore, a pole which had been made use of by the Nativs for lodge poles, & haul'd by dogs it is new and is a Certain Sign of the Indians being on the river above   a foot ball and Several other articles are also found to Substantiate this oppinion."

—William Clark, May 28, 1805

Crossroads in History

The 1803 Louisiana Purchase from France instantly doubled the size of the United States, although neither seller nor buyer had previously explored the property nor knew exactly where the boundaries were. And neither party considered that native peoples living there might have a valid claim of their own. Part of the mission for the Lewis and Clark Expedition was to appraise the new holdings and inform the occupants of their new leader in Washington.

Many tribes provided essential help to the Corps of Discovery, and the expedition would have failed without that kindness and generosity. Friendly or not, all tribes were later rounded up and effectively imprisoned on reservations. Two centuries later, many Native Americans understandably harbor deep resentment about colonization, genocide, and the loss of their land and liberty.

If Lewis and Clark symbolically opened the western frontier, the surrender of the Nez Perce (Nimmipu) near the Bear Paw Mountains in 1877 symbolically ended that frontier. Plagued by white depredations in their homeland, the Nimmipu struck out for Canada, eluding the U.S. Army for three months and 1,350 miles before being captured forty miles from the Canadian border.

Today, the Nez Perce National Historic Trail intersects the Lewis and Clark NHT at Cow Creek, part of today's Upper Missouri National Wild and Scenic River. The tribe crossed the river a week before their surrender.

Most people who float the wild and scenic river paddle only the first half to see the spectacular White Cliffs area, exiting at Judith Landing. Yet, the lower section to Cow Creek and beyond is equally or more stunning, featuring 800-foot-high stark hills of multi-toned mud and sandstone.

Bentonite clay swells when damp to create an impervious slippery layer, so that water runs off the land, not into the soil. Thus, the hills are largely desertified, except for pines and junipers rooted in bands of sandstone, plus the greasewood and grassland flats along the river.

Prairie Rose (Rosa arkansana)

We found the skeleton of a bighorn sheep.

Hiking up into the badlands from McGarry Bar.

71

Climbing the bluff in the early morning, I saw a herd of bighorn sheep grazing below, mere specks in this photo.

   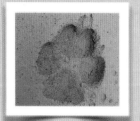 

Big horn sheep. Rush-skeleton plant (Lygodesmia juncea). Large concretions broken in half. Coyote track in the mud. Proceeding onward.

From Judith Landing we paddled to McGarry Bar, which was closed due to a bald eagle nesting site, so we camped a quarter-mile downstream. An afternoon hike into the badlands provided a great opportunity for botanizing and bird watching.

Concretions form almost like pearls as layers are build up around a nuclei.

Western meadowlarks serenaded our explorations. Song sparrows were common in the greasewood and sagebrush. I saw a western bluebird with its blue head, blue back, and orange vest. Cicadas chirped from every bush. Climbing up to the Douglas firs and junipers, we were greeted by red-breasted nuthatches coming curiously close to our party.

Even prickly pear cacti need protection.

Climbing the clay hills is like exploring a battlefield of craters, sinkholes formed where water tunnels into the bentonite to emerge again downslope. History forms in layers here, the silts and sands of an ancient sea bed. A thick rock of compressed clam shells tells the story of ages without time. The recent skeleton of a bighorn sheep, it's skull and horns intact, adds a new layer to the story.

In the morning I climbed to the top of the bluff and looked down on a herd of twenty bighorn sheep grazing near McGarry Bar. The Corps of Discovery hunted several bighorn sheep in this area, which Lewis described in detail their similarities and differences from domesticated sheep and goats. He noted that the animals preferred habitat is *"the cranies or crevices of the rocks in the faces of inacessible precepices, where the wolf nor bear*

Abandoned homestead cabin at Cow Creek.

A morning walk brought me up Cow Creek to another old cabin on land now managed by the American Prairie Reserve.

can reach them and where inddeed man himself would in many instancies find a similar deficiency; yet these animals bound from rock to rock and stand apparently in the most careless manner on the sides of precipices of many hundred feet."

A juvenile meadowlark sits still for camouflage.

Plains Pricklypear (Opuntia polyacantha).

Continuing downstream to Bullwhacker Creek, we observed damage from the ice dam formed during the spring thaw that backed the river up far beyond normal flood levels. Cottonwood trees high above the river were debarked up to eight-feet on the upstream side, evidently the work of moving icebergs. The campsite fence was demolished, the circular fire grate twisted beyond repair.

Finally we arrived at Cow Creek and camped for two nights at the crossroads of the two historic trails. We expected to live largely off dry goods for this stretch of the river until Josiah bought a secondhand cooler in Fort Benton and went full-tilt Lewis and Clark on red meat. We've eaten burger and steaks twice daily for a week, often made into burritos with cheese and wild greens. Life is good for our Missouri River Corps of Rediscovery.

Some people celebrate Lewis and Clark as famous explorers. Others condemn them as the leading edge of colonization and the usurping of Native American land and rights. I judge them as men of their time, bound by the beliefs and customs of the day.

Little would change if Lewis and Clark were somehow erased from time. History would have largely unfolded exactly as it did, except that we would be short a million words of first-hand documentation from their extensive journaling of the West prior to colonization.

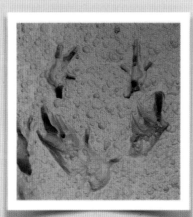

Frog or toad tracks.

Female Brewer's blackbird.

Morning sunlight from the top of the bluffs near Cow Creek.

Charles M. Russell National Wildlife Refuge

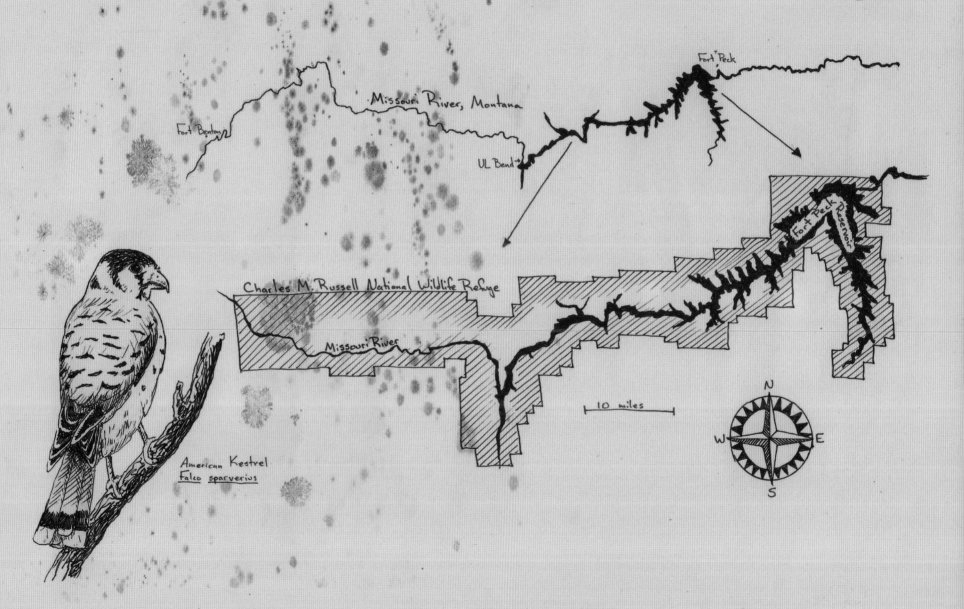

Fort Peck

Missouri River, Montana

Fort Benton

UL Bend

Charles M. Russell National Wildlife Refuge

Fort Peck Reservoir

Missouri River

10 miles

American Kestrel
Falco sparverius

N
W E
S

Fog rises at James Kipp Recreation Area.

"I walked on shore this morning   the country is not so broken as yesterday, tho' still high and roling or wavy; the hills on the Lard. side possess more pine than usual; some also on the Stard. hills. Salts and other mineral appearances as usual. the river continues about the same width or from 200 or 250 yds. wide, fewer sandbars and the courant more gentle and regular."

—Meriwether Lewis, May 22, 1805

Roaming and Rambling

Lewis and Clark frequently traded duties, one man overseeing the laborious push of canoes and pirogues up the Missouri, the other walking overland to explore, hunt, and observe the surrounding countryside. There were no fences, property lines, or "No Trespassing" signs. That freedom to roam remained the rule here in Montana for 200 years.

Trappers, traders, gold seekers, homesteaders, and cattlemen traversed Montana in every direction by foot and horseback. The tradition of open access continued after the fences went up. That was the world I knew as a youth, hopping across fences like they weren't there. In 1988, at twenty years old, my girlfriend and I walked 500 miles across Montana from my grandmother's house in Pony to Fort Union on the North Dakota border. Much of the route paralleled or intersected our present journey by water.

We had first walked across private farm fields from Pony to Three Forks, then followed an active railroad down the Missouri to Sixteen Mile Creek. Our map still showed the tracks of the former Chicago Milwaukee Railroad ascending Sixteen Mile, but we found the tracks removed and the path blocked by a locked gate plastered with No Trespassing signs.

I understood the words well enough, but the idea was incomprehensible to the free-roaming lifestyle I'd grown up with. Not having anywhere else to go, we climbed over the gate and followed the railbed upstream over wooden trestles and

Sow thistle (Sonchus arvensis) leaves are a favorite salad green here.

through convenient tunnels. We saw 28 elk and 250 deer in one day. The property manager found us camped by the creek, but fortunately decided we were harmless enough and let us continue our journey. It probably helped that we were two innocent young adults on an epic quest, with me wearing buckskin clothes and a rawhide backpack.

We followed the railbed, most of it private land, through Ringling, Martinsdale, and Two Dot to Harlowton, then went cross country across more farms and ranches through Judith Gap to Lewistown, north to Roy and crossed the Missouri River here at the Fred Robinson Bridge. Then we walked east through the Charles M. Russell National Wildlife Refuge, paralleling our present course down the river.

When newcomers tried to claim rivers and streams as their personal private property, fishermen took them to court arguing that Montana's rivers and

Hard at work kicking back with the sail.

A lovely spot, but thick with mosquitos.

The hills are abloom with invasive yellow sweet clover.

Calm evening waters.

Fireweed (Chamaenerion angustifolium) is usually found in the mountains, but there were patches in the wildlife refuge.

streams had always been public thoroughfares, and the courts agreed, leading to some of the strongest stream access laws in the country.

Sadly, nobody stood up for the similar right to roam the open countryside. When No Trespassing signs went up, walkers grudging shifted to non-posted parcels until those too were bought up by outsiders and closed to the world.

Fencing people out is effectively the same as fencing them in like cattle. A person who cannot walk out the door across an open field is living in a cage.

Zoo animals are known to have severe psychological disorders from living in cages. Cages impact people too. I've seen it in young adults at Green University LLC who ranted against the trap of civilization. Yet they were so conditioned to cages that they wouldn't think to leave the property to explore the 100,000 acres of adjacent public lands—unless I initiated the invitation to go for a hike.

Like my horse who would pace back and forth along an invisible fence after I removed the electric wire and plastic posts, these young people were controlled by fences even when there were none.

Having grown up without such limitations, I felt free to pursue all my dreams in life without credentials, certification, or jumping through hoops to get there. I built my own passive solar stone and log house without a mortgage, did my own plumbing and wiring, stared at blank pages long enough to launch a successful writing career and publishing company, and learned HTML without a manual. I am a slow learner, but unbounded by limitations. A vision or goal may require a dozen years of incubation to get airborne, as was the case with the Jefferson River Canoe Trail before we successfully bought our first campsite for the public.

Scott caught a beautiful catfish.

John batter-fried the catfish.

Wolf spider (Hogna sp.)

Tall blue lettuce (Lactuca biennis)

A spiny softshell turtle (Apalone spinifera) got caught on our set lines. We set it free.

I worry about the future for our young people who have known only cages. Freedom to roam is critical to inspire a new generation of thinkers, doers, and leaders. How will people think outside the box to solve humanity's most pressing problems if they've grown up boxed in by No Trespassing signs?

Ripe gooseberries (Ribes oxyacanthoides)

As I wrote these lines in bed in my tent in the rain, I reflected back on that walk across Montana thirty-one years ago. That was a drought year, the year Yellowstone burned. The grass never turned green in eastern Montana, but went "crunch, crunch" under our shoes." The hottest day was 110°F.

This year we were blessed with unusually cool, cloudy weather and plenty of rain. We found the wildlife refuge shockingly green. I named our campsite Spider Wash due to the abundance of gigantic wolf spiders and the abundance of runoff coming down the coulee. Scott caught a 27-inch channel catfish. He and John cooked a fabulous dinner of fish and chips while I gathered a salad of sow thistle leaves. We certainly didn't suffer for lack of food. We did, however, encounter our first significant mosquitoes.

Paddling into the morning sun.

Northern leopard frog. Historic survey marker. Prairie coneflower. We played Wildlife Web while waiting for lake winds to settle.

Wolf spider with dung ball.

Broomrape
(Orobanche ludoviciana)

Scott keeps reeling them in!

Night hawk chicks with near-perfect camouflage.

Looking out from the UL Bend National Wildlife Refuge.

"The country which borders the river is high broken and rocky, generally imbeded with a Soft Sand Stone. higher up the hill the Stone is of a brownish yellow hard and gritty... this Countrey may with propriety I think be termed the Deserts of America, as I do not Conceive any part can ever be Settled, as it is deficient in water, Timber & too Steep too be tilled."

—William Clark, May 26, 1805

Swiss Cheese and Bison

The Homestead Act of 1862 and various amendments allowed settlers to claim tracts of land and prove ownership by building a house and working the land. Settlers cherry-picked the most promising arable lands available. My grandfather August Elpel claimed land for the family homestead near Glendive, Montana in 1907.

Theodore Roosevelt set aside forested parcels as Forest Reserves, leading to creation of the U.S. Forest Service. Unclaimed lands were overseen by the General Land Office, which became the Bureau of Land Management in 1946.

The net result of the homestead movement was a Swiss cheese mix of private and public lands, typically shown on maps as white for private land with seemingly random blocks of yellow for public land, often without any physical public access.

The opposite is true along 300 miles of river and lake, from Fort Benton to Fort Peck, what William Clark described as the "Deserts of America." Here the maps are almost entirely yellow for BLM land, pock-marked with private inholdings where homesteaders claimed muddy creek bottoms between barren badlands.

It is here that the nonprofit American Prairie Reserve has been buying private inholdings with leases on adjacent public lands towards the goal of stitching together a 3 million-acre shortgrass prairie for a free-roaming bison herd. APR lands are open to public camping, hiking, and conditional hunting. We previously camped on APR land back at Cow Creek.

Seeing that APR's Buffalo Camp was within a few miles of Fort Peck Lake, I thought it might be the best opportunity during our 2,000-mile adventure to see actual bison as part of the Lewis and Clark National Historic Trail.

Sunrise over Scott's Old Town canoe.

We hiked overland in search of bison at the American Prairie Reserve. Catching a ride, we saw a dozen bison bulls grazing on BLM land.

I was also aware of rancher resentment of APR and the many roadside signs in prairie country stating, "Save a Cowboy, Stop American Prairie Reserve." I was curious to see APR for myself and get the inside scoop. I had neglected to initiate contact ahead of time, but serendipitously met a bird photographer back at the James Kipp Recreation Area who had just come from APR, and he provided inside contact information.

We took a layover day at Fourchette Creek Recreation Area to hike out in search of bison. Scott, John, and I followed a mosquito-infested coulee up through a ponderosa pine forest to attain cell service. We connected with Hila Shamoon of the Smithsonian Conservation Biology Institute, who was investigating how pasture size affects bison movement and behavior at APR. Hila graciously gave us a ride to the Enrico Education & Science Center. On the ride we saw a dozen big bison bulls grazing on BLM land. Hila explained that bulls separate from the herd in summer and often hang out together. APR's herd has grown from 16 bison in 2005 to nearly 1,000 animals today, with the ultimate goal of acquiring enough land to support 10,000 bison.

To fifth generation ranchers, restoring bison is an identity-level threat to an honorable way of life pioneered by their great-great grandparents. Rural towns have been shrinking for decades as young people move away in search of better opportunities. I've seen it in my own community where the K-12 school shrank from 125 students to 75 over twenty years. Revitalizing and repopulating our rural communities is one of the most neglected policy issues in Montana and beyond.

APR is perceived as exacerbating the problem by buying out family farms to raise bison. I peppered APR and Smithsonian field staff with dozens of questions, including the "Save a Cowboy" signs. They acknowledged the opposition and need for

*This lark sparrow nest has two chicks and an unhatched egg,
plus two speckled eggs laid by brown headed cowbirds.*

Lesser prairie chickens (Tympanuchus pallidicinctus).

better outreach and communication, but also recognized that big projects are often met with adversity until proven worthwhile. APR has already formed partnerships with some local ranchers, leasing APR land for cattle grazing and marketing "Wild Sky" grass-fed beef (www.wildskybeef.org) with profits benefiting local ranchers and the prairie project.

Wild bison traditionally grazed in massive herds, like those described by Lewis and Clark. Moving in tight bunches, they trampled seeds, grass, and brush into the soil, along with their own manure, effectively planting, mulching, and fertilizing the prairie to grow more grass. The grass absorbed carbon from the atmosphere while bison sequestered that carbon by trampling organic matter into the ground to build healthier soil. APR would like to restore traditional grazing patterns, but remains stymied by BLM grazing rules for cattle, which favor very few animals spread out over large acreage to minimize over-grazing.

Our arrival coincided with the end of an independently organized youth conservation camp at the education center. We received royal and unexpected treatment, including showers (our second since this journey began) and a hearty breakfast of biscuits and gravy and scrambled eggs. We watched an herbal medicine slideshow with the youth program, then checked email while they made soothing salves for insect bites.

As a botanist, I had fun geeking out about plants with Kimberly and Catherine from the Smithsonian Environmental Research Center who were doing baseline studies about prairie pasture species. I introduced my botany card game, and played *Memory, Slap Flower, Crazy Flowers*, and *Shanleya's Harvest*, based on my children's book, *Shanleya's Quest*.

Every stop offers an invitation to get out and hike into the prairie badlands.

Curlycup gumweed
(Grindelia squarrosa)

The crew graciously gave us a ride back to camp, sending us with leftover goodies from the youth camp, plus ice for the cooler and enough water to continue our journey across the lake.

While APR is the obvious target of the "Save a Cowboy" signs, I wondered if the impact was felt primarily by fellow ranchers who might be stigmatized for working with APR. For these families, there isn't a sixth generation that wants to stay and work the land, and selling out is not a question of "if" but "when." Selling out to APR is their best bet to obtain the retirement they've earned.

As for the bison, they were an integral part of the Lewis and Clark journey, repeatedly referred to in the journals. With world wildlife populations crashing, such that people and livestock make up 96% of all mammalian life, it doesn't seem unreasonable to give bison a narrow strip of land that Clark deemed otherwise unfit for settlement.

"Set out at sunrise and proceeded but a short distance ere the wind became so violent that we were obliged to come too, which we did on the Lard. side in a suddon or short bend of the river where we were in a great measure sheltered from the effects of the wind. the wind continued violent all day, the clouds were thick and black, had a slight sprinkle of rain several times during the course of the day."

—Meriwether Lewis, May 10, 1805

The Lakeness Monster

Preparing to fry walleye fish for dinner.

Meriwether Lewis penned his words from the bottom of what is now Fort Peck Lake, an immense, 130-mile-long reservoir in eastern Montana held back by a four-mile-long hydraulically filled earthen dam. The artificial lake fills badland coulees, creating a jagged 1,500-mile perimeter shoreline. The violent winds that sent Lewis and Clark for shelter now blow unfettered across the wide-open surface of the lake, amplifying the hazards. Fort Peck is known for it's sudden storms, tent-flattening winds, and six-foot waves that imperil motor boats.

I previously met a fellow camper who dragged his canoe fifty feet away from the

A gorgeous sunset followed a tent-flattening storm.

water, drove in a heavy stake, and lashed the canoe to the ground. "There is a man with experience," I thought to myself.

He explained that he once got caught in a storm on Peck where he and his partner barely made it back to shore, only to have the wind launch their aluminum canoe so high that it broke in half when it hit the ground.

Until this point, our journey was easy, drifting down the river like driving a scenic byway, occasionally applying the paddle to the water to accelerate through a section of slow current. Like a kid arriving at camp, I was always excited to run around exploring each temporary new home.

We were blessed with a never-ending bloom of wild roses and shockingly few mosquitoes. But any great adventure cannot be roses all the time. We finally reached the end of the flowing river and the end of the wild roses. It was time to face the Lakeness Monster.

Scott caught a monster northern pike.

A rare moment of placid water on Fort Peck Lake.

Compared to the river, paddling a big lake is like driving a fifty-lane highway in a vessel with no engine. Propulsion is achieved by stabbing ahead with a stick, pulling oneself forward an arm-length at a time. A landmark knob plainly visible ahead seemed tantalizingly close yet frustratingly far away as we spent hours mindlessly paddling towards the unattainable goal.

Motor boats were scarce, but occasionally zoomed by as if we are standing still, which we basically were. My paddle partner, John, and I barely spoke to each other, not out of animosity, but because the gentle "sploosh, sploosh" of the paddles was just loud enough to interfere with conversation. If we talked, we stopped paddling. If we stopped paddling, we stopped moving. And if there was a gentle breeze against us, we immediately drifted backwards.

Woodhouse's toad (Anaxyrus woodhousii)

Rainbows are the reward for weathering storms.

Fortunately, we received an updated ten-day forecast calling for clear skies and 80°F daily temperatures, a great reprieve from the succession of storms we weathered.

Our first sunny day turned cloudy and gray with light rain overnight. Our second sunny day was considerably darker, and the evening rain turned into a drencher that lasted halfway through the next day.

Fishing after the storm.

When we dried out and proceeded on a day later, we faced a headwind that drained our forward momentum. We abandoned the quest to wait out the wind.

The lake was characteristically calm in the evenings, so we paddled into the night, arriving at camp at 11 p.m. The next day we paddled from 9 a.m. to 9 p.m. covering twenty miles in one grueling long day.

If paddling the lake wasn't fun enough, we finally found the mosquitoes, biting flies, and no see ums. The landscape normally would have been parched dry, but was wetter and greener than locals could remember. More than green, the hills glowed with yellow sweet clover.

The least buggy place to stand was on the shoreline. Shade was rarely an option, and often too buggy. We were faced with the option of frying in the sun, baking in our tents, being eaten alive by bugs, or paddling until our arms fell off. Of course there was no place I would rather be.

Scott caught a huge walleye, "bigger than the ones I've seen mounted," he emphasized. Having caught and released numerous smaller fish, he called it his "best day fishing ever."

After our layover at Fourchette Bay, we paddled a fifteen-mile day followed by a tent-flattening storm during dinner and a gorgeous red sunset. Another day,

Blowing across the lake.

Waiting for wind and waves to calm down.

Nighthawk eggs, nearly invisible on bare ground.

Fort Peck Dam flooded badlands coulees, creating 1,500 miles of lakeshore, much of it in peninsulas like this.

93

Mineral dendrite formation on a baculite fossil.

Baculite fossil.

Concretions are common here, like natural cannonballs embedded in the badlands landscape.

another fifteen miles, this time blessed with a tail wind. Scott caught a 33-inch northern pike. He and Chris landed it with a net half the size of the fish. Dinner came with another tent-flattening storm followed by a stunning double rainbow.

Coming from Fort Benton, we've paddled up through 20 million years of geologic history to the 70 million-year-old Bearpaw Formation. The dark grey-brown shale erodes into soft, barren landforms of cracked mud and sparse vegetation. Large round concretions are common here, as are baculite and ammonite fossils. Baculites were primitive relatives of squid with straight, segmented shells.

Fossil collecting is illegal within the wildlife refuge, and realistically, who really needs fossils anyway? They could collect dust on a shelf, or remain on the ground to the delight of the next hiker or paddler to wander out into this remote country. Photographs are treasures enough for me.

We took a layover day at The Pines Recreation Area due to a high wind advisory. The community kitchen included an indoor shelter, electric stove, lights, and badly needed outlets to recharge our electronics.

Ammonite fossil.

A gophersnake blends in with Bearpaw shale.

Another beautiful sunset.

95

Montana / July 17 / Fort Peck Lake / Seventh Coulee Bay to The Pines

The recreation area is part of a lakeside pocket of forest in a sea of prairie, featuring ponderosa pine (*Pinus pondersoa*) intermixed with Rocky Mountain juniper (*Juniperus scopulorum*), common juniper (*J. communis*), and creeping juniper (*J. horizontalis*). For Lewis and Clark, this was the first time they encountered pines of any kind on the Missouri River, and the first time they had ever seen ponderosa pines. While I anticipated dried-up prairie, the continuing rains triggered a boom in mushrooms. Finding king bolete mushrooms (*Boletus edulis*) was as shocking as it was delightful. I usually find them in underneath spruce trees in moist soil near streams high in the mountains of western Montana. They made a fine meal.

Desert evening primrose (Oenothera caespitosa) blooms at sunset to be pollinated overnight by moths.

Thankfully, we paddled beyond the worst of the mosquitos, and the land was measurably drier than before. Beyond The Pines, we still had two more days of wind and waves, bobbing up and down like ships on the sea. As we crossed each bay from point to point, I continually worried that a big wind might rise up and blow us irretrievably across the lake. We waited out the worst of the winds and braved the rest, finally reaching Fort Peck Marina and Fort Peck Dam.

Adam finished his trip here, having paddled ahead since Cow Creek. He completed what many people consider the most scenic portion of the entire Missouri River. For the rest of us, Fort Peck marked the end of the beginning. We still had a looong way to go!

Sunning on the lake.

Community shelter at The Pines Recreation Area.

Purple prairie clover (Dalea purpurea).

Whorled milkweed (Asclepias verticillata).

Scott and Chris team up to flip a pancake with forks, for lack of a proper spatula.

97

Ponderosa pine cones and reindeer lichen (Cladonia arbuscula).

Yellow-flowered alfalfa
(Medicago sativa subsp. falcata).

Russula mushroom (Russula sp.)

Sunset viewed from The Pines Recreation Area.

Ponderosa skeleton silhouetted against the evening sky.

Wild sunflower (Helianthus annuus) backlit by the sunlight.

Queen Alexandra's sulphur (Colias alexandra).

Scott has fed us well on Fort Peck Lake!

Whitetail deer antler.

Sometimes the wind does most of the work as we drift across the lake.

Wild sunflower.

I found a nice bunch of king bolete mushrooms (Boletus edulis), which made a great addition to our evening meal.

Photo by Scott Robinson

A lone island protrudes from the lake, the tip of a submerged ridge line that otherwise separates one coulee from another.

Deer tracks follow the peninsula.

Photo by Scott Robinson

Home is where the canoe is.

A flower beetle on a wild sunflower.

Col. Campbell K. Peck

Colonel Campbell K. Peck likely never visited Montana, yet his footprint looms large in his namesake town, reservation, dam, and lake. Peck partnered with Elias H. Durfee to form the trading firm of Durfee and Peck in Leavenworth, Kansas. An employee constructed Fort Peck in 1867 to trade with the Assiniboine and Sioux tribes. Fort Peck became an Indian Agency from 1873 until 1878, but was moved downstream to Poplar due to repeated flooding at the original site. The Fort Peck Reservation was negotiated over the winter of 1886-87 and ratified in 1888, establishing its present boundaries.

In 1933, the Army Corps of Engineers began construction of Fort Peck Dam near the original fort site. A new town of Fort Peck was built two miles north of the fort site to house construction workers.

We loaded the canoes on the trailer to portage around Fort Peck Dam

Indoor fort at the Children's Museum.

Headed to Glasgow for a day on the town.

The Children's Museum of Glasgow hosts
the Skip Erickson World Wildlife Exhibit.

103

Jeff and Becky Blend helped us portage.

"We nooned it just above the entrance of a large river which disimbogues on the Lard. side; I took advantage of this leisure moment and examined the river about 3 miles; I found it generally 150 yards wide, and in some places 200. it is deep, gentle in it's courant and affords a large boddy of water; it's banks which are formed of a dark rich loam and blue clay are abbrupt and about 12 feet high. it's bed is principally mud... the water of the river possesses a peculiar whiteness, being about the colour of a cup of tea with the admixture of a tablespoonfull of milk. from the colour of it's water we called it Milk river."

—Meriwether Lewis, May 8, 1805

Name Games

The Missouri that emerges below Fort Peck Dam is not the same river we paddled into the lake nearly two weeks earlier. Above the lake, the Missouri is coffee-colored, knee-deep with mud, and barely cool. Sediment settles into the lake, and deep water becomes progressively clearer and colder towards the dam. Below the dam, the water is crystal clear, blue-tinted, and frigid cold, straight off the bottom of the lake. While much of the country sweltered under a heat wave, we paddled away our first 95°F days enjoying a chilly breeze off the water, like driving a car with the windows open and the air conditioner cranked.

Soon we reached the confluence with the Milk River, where fresh sediment pours into the Missouri. A narrow stream of cream mixes with the wider stream of aqua blue for several miles until visibility subsides and the river takes on a greenish-murky hue.

As mentioned previously, the Milk River was the Missouri until Ice Age glaciers shoved the river south to carve a new channel and create the rugged, scenic badlands we've enjoyed so much since Fort Benton. In rejoining it's historical channel, the Missouri becomes a prairie river again, meandering back and forth in great cottonwood-lined loops, intermittently bumping up against higher badlands to the south.

The Milk River was known by the Mandans as "Ah-mâh-tâh, cu-shush-sur" or "The River that Scolds at All Others." Lewis rejected that name in favor

Blue water from the Missouri mixes with cloudy water from the Milk River downstream from the confluence.

of his westernized alternative. However, many Indian names have persisted over time, including Missouri, Kansas, Iowa, and Dakota. There were also names from French Canadian trappers, which Americans typically translated into English, such as the "Roche Jaune," which became the Yellow Stone or Yellowstone River.

Lewis and Clark ascended the Missouri naming nearly every creek and river after members of their expedition, prominent politicians in Washington, natural features, and potential girlfriends back home. Names for the larger tributaries have mostly remained in use while names for smaller streams were often forgotten and renamed by later trappers and settlers.

I have also played the name game, naming isolated parcels of BLM land as campsites on the Jefferson River Canoe Trail. I considered tackling a similar project on the Missouri to create the "Big Muddy National Water Trail." It would be the water equivalent of the Appalachian Trail, but with about 1% as many travelers.

Hairy evening-primrose (Oenothera villosa)

The project would have entailed visiting, photographing, and describing every existing campsite on the Missouri, as well as similarly evaluating and naming every scrap of BLM and other public land for its campsite potential to create an online map with GPS coordinates for others to follow. That was a bigger project than I desired, choosing instead to plant the idea for someone else to pursue.

For the sake of example, I decided to name some parcels otherwise marked in my notes as "BLM South 1, 2, 3" etc., the parcels being on the south side of the river, opposite the Fort Peck Indian Reservation.

The first BLM site featured clay-capped badlands with several square miles of public lands for hiking and exploring. In recognition of French heritage, I named the campsite "Pomme Blanche," meaning "white apple," a name cited by Lewis when describing a Pea family plant otherwise known as "breadroot" (*Psoralea esculenta*).

A gopher snake tried boarding the canoe until Scott pushed it off with his paddle.

Baculite fossils are common on the prairie.

After lallygagging our way across most of Montana, we started paddling longer distances, taking advantage of unusually high water levels and blessed tail winds to cover 20 to 25 miles per day.

We stopped at Wolf Point to cook lunch while Josiah and Chris walked into town for ice. After a longer than expected absence, they returned with ice and a stray puppy, explaining the process by which they reasonably concluded it was abandoned. Chris named her Jubilee, the newest and youngest member of the Missouri River Corps of Rediscovery.

The Fort Peck Reservation is 125 miles long as the crow flies, somewhat longer following the looping course of the Missouri. Fort Peck is home to the Sisseton, Wahpetons, Yanktonais, and Teton Hunkpapa divisions of the Sioux Nation as well as the Canoe Paddler and Red Bottom bands of the Assiniboine Nation. Although separate, Sioux and Assiniboine have similar-sounding languages of the Siouan language family.

Ospreys were common near the clear water below Fort Peck Dam, but disappeared as the river progressively regained turbidity, reducing subsurface visibility for these aerial predators.

Each bend in the river is a mile-long loop around a peninsula, the banks characteristically muddy. Bald eagles somehow manage to hunt the opaque waters. Red-tailed hawks dominated for a stretch, presumably hunting prairie rodents nearby.

We camped at a parcel of BLM land with three irrigation pumps loudly pumping water out of the river into an irrigation ditch on the side of the hill. I named the site Triple Pump, and we camped as far away as possible from the noise.

Leaving camp, we paddle out a narrow slough back to the main river channel.

Deer bed overlooking the river.

Northern leopard frogs are abundant here.

A fragile clam fossil.

Cicer milkvetch (Astragalus cicer)

Mourning dove nest.

Sunset over the prairie river.

Fewflower buckwheat (Eriogonum pauciflorum)

Chris and Jubilee, proud papa, happy puppy.

*White-lined sphinx
(Hyles lineata)*

*Sagebrush smoke mosquito
repellant in rotten log.*

Continuing downriver, we encountered our first purple coneflower (*Echinacea*). The land was as green as the month of June thanks to all the rain, the second highest runoff year in the Missouri basin since record-keeping began. We stopped at Lewis and Clark Park for the afternoon, but since it was closed to camping, we paddled downstream to camp on private land.

The next day we camped at an unusually lush parcel of BLM land at the mouth of the Redwater River, which Lewis and Clark originally named "2,000-mile Creek," their approximate distance up the Missouri River. The Missouri is much shorter now that the lower portions have been straightened and deepened by the U.S. Army Corps of Engineers. I named the campsite Redwater out of intuitive simplicity.

Cottonwoods lean away for equal space.

Black "golden" currants
(Ribes aurem)

Purple coneflower
(Echinacea angustifolia)

Look close. Toad in deer track.

Plains spade foot toad
(Spea bombifrons)

We moored our canoes in a small bay off the Missouri River at Redwater.

Sailing down the river.

Sweet puppy Jubilee.

*Prairie coneflower
(Ratibida columnifera)*

John checks out an overhanging rock.

Connected concretions look like a giant fossilized pea pod.

My favorite stop was a parcel of public land known as Mortarstone Bluff with extensive badlands formations, including eroded clay hills and bluffs, sandstone outcroppings, and weirdly shaped concretions. We took a layover day to hike and explore the area. Sites like this are public treasures that most people just paddle on by. Without recognition, such sites remain susceptible to mining, drilling, or other plunder. I hope Mortarstone Bluff will one day see protection as a campsite on the Big Muddy segment of the Lewis and Clark National Historic Trail. I do not know whether anyone else will use or remember these sites, but I hope to at least plant the seeds for an official Big Muddy National Water Trail.

Evening sun lights up the badlands at Mortarstone Bluff.

Morning fog settles on the Missouri River.

Mule deer skull in the badlands.

Narrow ridge in the badlands.

Clay seals to shed water, preventing vegetation.

*Western spiderwort
(Tradescantia occidentalis)*

Spooked deer.

Scott, Josiah, John, and I enjoyed an early morning hike into the badlands.

113

"We came too this evening in the mouth of a little river, which falls in on the Stard. side. This stream is about 50 yards wide from bank to bank; the water occupyes about 15 yards. the banks are of earth only, abrupt, 'tho not high— the bed is of mud principally. Capt Clark, who was up this stream about three miles, informed me that it continued about the same width, that it's current was gentle and it appeared navigable for perogues... This stream my friend Capt. C. named Marthas river."

—*Meriwether Lewis, April 29, 1805*

Creatures of the Mud

Mud. It defines our existence as the boundary between water and land. Mud is the event horizon separating the universe of wet from the universe of dry. To cross the threshold in either direction we must become creatures of the mud.

How many times have I stood on dry land with clean feet, staring at my canoe moored in the mire only a few feet away? No matter how well organized we may be, there is always some small item needed from the canoes that requires yet another trip through the mud. I wonder how the men of the Lewis and Clark Expedition managed to cope with it all the time.

Mud is a way of life on the "Big Muddy" Missouri River.

While we camp on land, our canoes remain in the mud, especially my heavy dugout canoe. It is like living with a moat of mud bisecting one's house, where the kitchen stove is on one side of the moat, while the fridge, pantry, and sink are on the other, where our bedrooms are separated from our dressers, where the bathtub can only be accessed by wading through the mud both before and afterwards. Doing laundry, either in the river or rarely in town, is a futile effort for creatures of the mud.

In the upper reaches of the Missouri, the mud was black, rich with organic matter, and typically only an inch or two deep, yet the problem was fundamentally similar. Sloshing around in sandals is fine, except that the constant dampness ultimately dried out my skin, causing deep, painful cracks beneath the

114

toes. Barefoot is ideal to wade in and out and dry quickly, but not pain-free where the shore is covered with spiky cockleburs.

Repairing cracked feet requires diligent care to keep them clean and dry, applying lotion and clean socks and shoes until the skin knits back together. Yet, the moment one successfully finishes putting on dry shoes is invariably the moment something else is needed from the canoe.

Coping with mud is like enduring Chinese water torture: a slow drip of water on the forehead may be utterly harmless, yet keep it up long enough and a person will go utterly mad. At no point is the mud truly debilitating, yet like water torture, or mosquitos buzzing about one's ear, how long can anyone endure a persistently minor annoyance?

The Missouri breaks have a special kind of mud, consisting of fine clay particles that make up gumbo, mud so sticky that it immediately cakes up thickly on shoes or tires, rendering walking or driving impossible after a rain.

Climbing the bluff at sunrise.

Wild bergamot or horsemint (Monarda fistulosa).

115

In wet or dry weather, that gumbo forms an imposing barrier between the river and land. At some campsites we slogged barefoot back and forth through fifty feet of soupy gumbo that would suck any footwear right off our feet. There is a reason the Missouri is known as the "Big Muddy."

We were pleasantly surprised that the mud largely disappeared through Fort Peck Lake where the shores consist of crumbly shale. Below the dam, the river is initially silt-free with sandy shorelines. However, it didn't take long for the river to re-assert itself and we again became creatures of the mud.

Scott and I enjoyed a scenic morning hike, here overlooking recently-harvested barley fields.

Continuing downstream, the landscape is less dominated by badlands clay, giving way to sandy bluffs instead. As elsewhere, any topography unsuitable for farming was typically bypassed by settlers, which aids in identifying blocks of public land.

Sacagawea showed William Clark the yellow flowers of the golden currant (*Ribes aurem*) near here on April 30th, 1805. We enjoyed the fruits of those flowers on our journey of rediscovery, each day later in our summer becoming a day earlier in their spring as we travel backwards through their journals. Although known as a golden currant, this is a black-fruited subspecies, with bigger, more tasty fruits than the golden currants I know at home. At camp, I tossed driftwood onto the shallow mud to make a rare and cherished dry path to the dugout canoe.

The next day we stopped for lunch at the confluence of Marthas River, now known as Big Muddy Creek, the eastern boundary of the Fort Peck Reservation. Most creeks in eastern Montana could be named either Big or Little Muddy Creek, yet here the shore was delightfully sandy.

Photo by Scott Robinson

Pelicans gather on and around a fallen tree.

I found agates in the imported roadbed gravel.

117

Prairie Rattlesnake (Crotalus viridis)

Camping at another block of BLM land near Culbertson, Montana, we walked a dirt road, picking agates out of the gravel used to surface the roadbed.

We saw two rattlesnakes, the first of our trip. Rattlesnakes were common for Lewis and Clark, and a major concern for us as we walked through deep grass barefoot or in sandals, yet rattlesnakes throughout Montana have become alarmingly scarce.

Here the soil is dominated by sand, and the river is too. Still we must slog through a foot of mud beneath the water, wading carefully forward, feeling for the edge, trying to discern if we can safely dive in without plunging face-first into a submerged stick, rock, or the gaping jaws of a long lost plesiosaur. Who knows what really lies beneath these murky waters?

For our final night in Montana, we pitched our tents on the beach of a mosquito-infested riparian woodland, a wholly appropriate camp in honor of William Clark's 249th birthday. Overall, we had relatively few mosquitos, but sometimes they were persistent to horrendous. Writing from my tent during a passing storm, my feet lay out the unzipped door, my toes encrusted with globs of half-dried mud. Thinking back to Lewis and Clark, I'm sure they lived as we do, as creatures of the mud.

The Missouri River remains wild and scenic far beyond the official Wild and Scenic designation.

North Dakota

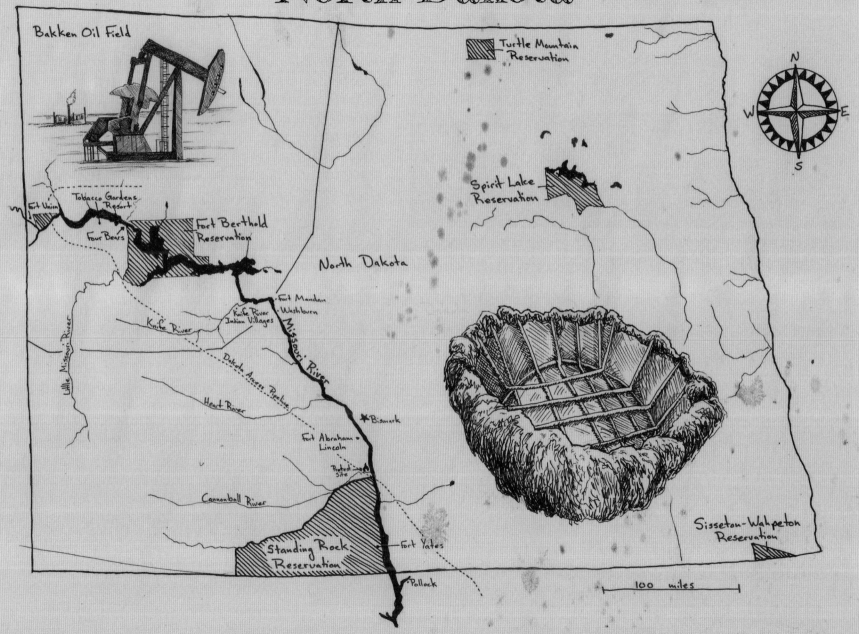

Bakken Oil Field

Turtle Mountain
Reservation

Spirit Lake
Reservation

Ft Union

Tobacco Gardens
Resort

Four Bears

Fort Berthold
Reservation

North Dakota

Fort Mandan
Washburn

Knife River
Indian Villages

Knife River

Little Missouri River

Missouri River

Dakota Access Pipeline

Heart River

★ Bismark

Fort Abraham
Lincoln

Protest
Site

Cannonball River

Standing Rock
Reservation

Fort Yates

Pollock

Sisseton-Wahpeton
Reservation

100 miles

"Capt Clark thinks that the lower extremity of the low plane would be most eligible for this establishment; it is true that it is much nearer both rivers, and might answer very well, but I think it reather too low to venture a permanent establishment, particularly if built of brick or other durable materials, at any considerable expence; for so capricious, and versatile are these rivers, that it is difficult to say how long it will be, untill they direct the force of their currents against this narrow part of the low plain, which when they do, must shortly yeald to their influence; in such case a few years only would be necessary, for the annihilation of the plain, and with it the fortification."

—Meriwether Lewis, April 27, 1805

The Bourgeois House at Fort Union was residence to the trading post manager.

Confluence

Defensive bastions protected opposite corners of Fort Union.

Before there were railroads and highways there were rivers. Navigable rivers were thoroughfares of travel and commerce, so Lewis and Clark noted potential sites for forts and settlements along the Missouri. The junction of two major rivers was of particular interest to early American expansion, so both captains evaluated the confluence of the Yellowstone and Missouri rivers with an eye for future "establishments." In a rare rebuke of his co-captain, Lewis noted that Clark's site suggestion was a lousy idea.

Twenty-three years later, the American Fur Company constructed its Fort Union Trading Post three miles up the Missouri on a high bluff with access to a deep port for boats by the front gate. The company imported wares from Europe, Asia, and the American colonies, including beads, cookware, guns, knives, blankets, cloth, and alcohol, which were traded for furs and buffalo robes from regional tribes. Fort Union exported $100,000 in furs and hides annually to world markets, staying in business from 1828 to 1867.

Fort Union was then sold to the U.S. Army and dismantled for materials to expand Fort Buford closer to the confluence. Fort Union as it exists today was rebuilt based on artist sketches and archaeological excavations of its foundations. The stately "Bourgeios House" was completed before our 500-mile walk across Montana in 1988, while the palisade walls and bastions were reconstructed later.

In a confluence of past and present, paddling 700 miles to Fort Union brackets the major events of my life. The walk across Montana was undertaken before marriage and family, while the present journey by canoe comes post-divorce and as an empty-nester. I've explored the western states extensively, but never east. Fort Union lay on the Montana-North Dakota border. Everything beyond was a new frontier, fitting for this new era of my life.

Sawyer provided us with a "letter of introduction" to deliver to American Fur Company headquarters in St. Louis.

Over time the Missouri River has shifted so far south that the fort is largely inaccessible by water, so we tied our canoes downstream and walked two miles back by road. We were heartily greeted by the staff and enjoyed a lazy afternoon learning about the fort while recharging cameras and phones. They graciously gave us a ride back to the canoes after closing. As we paddled away, Sawyer, the site historian and re-enactor, came running to the river bank with mail: a letter of introduction written in pen and ink for us to deliver to American Fur Company headquarters in St. Louis, "if they are still in business..."

Sawyer showed us the trade room where trades were negotiated.

"A letter of introduction for Mr. Pierre Chouteau. These fine men are most able-bodied canoers and tried and true men of the river. Each has stopped at Fort Union and made himself and his good character known. Where they came is some great distance, and has fully served as a test to their employability with the Company as promising rivermen at $345 per annum.

Your unwavering servant, Sawyer R. F."

Riverside break and confab.

Engraved bench at the interpretive center.

We paddled downriver to the Missouri-Yellowstone Confluence Interpretive Center and campground. The water was deceptively placid, and paddling the Missouri often felt like paddling a long lake more than a big river, yet the current typically moved at 2 to 4 miles per hour, bringing submerged trees into the path faster than anticipated.

Another day of paddling brought us to Trenton Lake, formed from an old bend of the Missouri, but still accessible through a narrow channel. Although this year was unusually wet, we were behind the floodwaters until now. Here the river had recently dropped four feet, yet remained a foot above flood stage. We encountered deep mud and the worst mosquitos of the entire trip.

Confluence. The Missouri (right) is joined by the Yellowstone (upper left), continuing downstream as a bigger Missouri River (lower left).

We camped and joined a community pow wow hosted by the Turtle Mountain Chippewa. We were welcomed like family to the dinner and dances. John and I joined the potato dance where partners place a potato between their foreheads and dance until losing the potato. Dusty and I made it to third place. Anita and Brett Williamson sent us with a pouch of tobacco containing the community's prayers to accompany our journey downriver.

A cottonwood snag lie moored in the river.

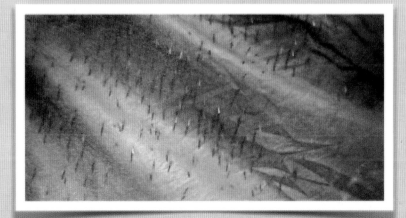

This was the night of the entire trip for mosquitos!

Dancers at the community pow wow.

We were joined by Charles Tatch, who drove up from Georgia to paddle with our expedition for a week. Thick willows and thicker mosquitoes limited campsite opportunities, so we paddled down to the fishing access at Lewis and Clark Bridge on Highway 85.

Receding floodwaters left deep mud behind.

The quiet energy of the merged Yellowstone and Missouri rivers gave way to its confluence with commerce. Oil rigs sprouted up beside the river, and oil trains rumbled by, laying on the horn. Trucks and cars roared over the bridge. Helicopters buzzed overhead. As if attracted to all the energy, a storm rolled in at nightfall, adding lightning, thunder, wind, and rain to the commotion.

That was a lot of noise for a crew that just spent six weeks paddling through one of the most remote, least-populated sections of the lower forty-eight states. Yet it was all part of the experience for the Missouri River Corps of Rediscovery on our continuing journey to explore the river from Three Forks, Montana to St. Louis, Missouri.

Chris and Scott paddle the Old Town on a sunny summer evening.

*Prickly lettuce blossoms
(Lactuca canadensis)*

"The whol face of the country was covered with herds of Elk & Antelopes; deer are also abundant, but keep themselves more concealed in the woodland. the buffalo Elk and Antelope are so gentle that we pass near them while feeding, without apearing to excite any alarm among them, and when we attract their attention, they frequently approach us more nearly to discover what we are, and in some instances pursue us a considerable distance apparently with that view."

—Meriwether Lewis, April 25, 1805

Bones and Oil

Hunters of the Corps of Discovery primarily conserved lead and gun powder for big game to feed the most men with the least resources. During the 28-month expedition they killed and ate 1,001 deer, 375 elk, 227 bison, 62 antelope, 35 bighorn sheep, 43 grizzly bears, 23 black bears, 113 beaver, 16 otters, 104 geese and brant, 46 grouse, 9 turkeys, 48 plovers, a number of horses and dogs, plus 18 wolves, of which they only ate one.

Although the men were voracious predators, the impact of the expedition was negligible compared to the predator that followed in their wake: commerce. In exchange for trade goods, Whites and Indians systematically trapped every beaver, muskrat, and other marketable fur they could obtain. Meat was often discarded as a by-product in the quest for furs.

There was also a market for buffalo hides, primarily used as belts for machinery in the

Dandelion leaves and currant berry salad.

Ashcakes were cooked on the hot coals, then returned to the pan to cool.

125

Oil rigs on the hill are eerily suggestive of Easter Island statues.

Natural gas is burned off for disposal.

emerging industrial revolution. Buffalo meat, however, had zero value since there was no practical means to transport it to market. Whole bison were left to rot on the prairie, killed only for their hides.

Railroads brought more commerce. Railroad companies encouraged passengers to shoot bison to prevent their blocking the tracks. They advertised bison shooting as a sport, much as people still shoot ground squirrels and prairie dogs for entertainment.

Cattlemen sought to eliminate bison to make room for livestock, and the U.S. Army favored culling bison to eliminate the primary food supply of the Indians, ultimately forcing them onto reservations. Millions of bison were left to rot on the prairie, their bleached bones later collected and ground up for sale as fertilizer.

As a beneficiary of the market economy, I am keenly aware that commerce provides unprecedented innovation and material wealth. We are privileged to choose our own paths in life, including having the opportunity to paddle the river. That's the irony of it, the forces that allow our Missouri River Corps of Rediscovery to exist are the same forces that plant oil wells along the Missouri River in western North Dakota.

As seen from the water, the roads and pads are not visible, so the oil wells seem to sprout from the land itself. Like mushrooms popping out of the soil, there are oil rigs everywhere, lining the riverbank, sprouting from hay fields and badlands, or silhouetted on the rim against the sky. There are traditional oil rigs and newer square columns that look eerily suggestive of Easter Island

Charles preferred paddling from the front.

Oil wells and gas flares sprouted from hay fields.

statues, the classic symbol of a culture that overshot its resource base and collapsed.

At nearly every oil pad is a flame, burning off natural gas to separate it from the oil. It isn't that the gas isn't useful, but like tens of millions of bison carcasses on the prairie, the resource has zero value in the absence of any infrastructure to bring it to market.

Nap time.

Saudi Arabia previously torched enough natural gas to supply the world for 400 years because they lacked the means to bring it to market. On a smaller scale, North Dakota flares off enough natural gas to heat tens of millions of homes. Although western North Dakota is rural, the light of so many flares makes the western part of the state as bright as Chicago at night when viewed from space. Wherever we paddle, wherever we hike, we are encircled by oil rigs and gas flares, some flames reaching 50 to 100 feet in height and audible from three miles away, like a passing jet engine that never actually goes anywhere.

With all the rain this year, the land remains as green as spring. The random intermingling of prairie, hills, hayfields, oil wells, and gas flares creates a peculiar illusion, like some kind of video game. Where else would you see fire randomly spouting from the hills, but in a video game full of sorcerers and magic?

Lake Sakakawea was greener than I imagined.

Gas pipelines are slowly being installed to capture natural gas instead of wasting it, yet no oil company is going to cease operations and stop flaring in the meantime.

As a young man, I was drawn to the work of Amory Lovins, one of the top energy experts in the world. Lovins demonstrated that we could avoid global warming at a net profit by investing in conservation measures for less than it cost to produce energy. Market forces could be harnessed to make the world a better place, a model I have subscribed to through my personal life and career. Applying a conservation ethic is one of the main reasons I could afford to follow my dreams in life, including spending six months paddling the Missouri.

This one gas flare is more than fifty feet long, burning twenty-four hours per day.

Thus it was shocking to witness such flagrant resource waste, emphasizing the fundamental unsolved problem of the market economy— that the future has no value. There is no incentive to conserve resources for the next generation or even ensure that there is a next generation. Like the statues of Easter Island, the oil rigs overlooking the river could easily become monuments to yet another culture that overshot its resource base and collapsed.

"Set out at an early hour this morning. about nine A. M. the wind arose, and shortly after became so violent that we were unable to proceed, in short it was with much difficulty and some risk that I was enabled to get the canoes and perogues into a place of tolerable safety, there being no timber on either side of the river at this place. some of the canoes shiped water, and wet several parsels of their lading, which I directed to be opened and aired   we remained untill five in the evening when the wind abating in some measure, we reloaded and proceeded."

—Meriwether Lewis, April 23, 1805

Sunrise over Lake Sakakawea.

Angels

There were no lakes on the Missouri when Lewis and Clark ascended it in 1804 and 1805. Now there are fifteen dams creating 700 miles of reservoir. It is the equivalent of paddling from Seattle to San Francisco on a lake, except that, like the ocean, big lakes are seldom calm. The wind ceaselessly blows from one direction or another. For an expedition of small canoes on big water, we depend on angels to carry us through.

I knew we could handle Fort Peck Lake (134 miles). It was Lake Sakakawea (178 miles) and Lake Oahe (231 miles) that really concerned me during the planning phase. If our goal were merely to paddle, then we could push forward inch by inch, stabbing at the water with our paddles 100,000+ times to get across Sakakawea and more to overcome Oahe. However, there seemed little to gain from the experience beyond repetitive stress injuries. I mulled over various alternatives, but never came up with a plan beyond hoping for Divine Intervention.

We've been helped by many Angels on the journey, notably my mother and sister and aunt and uncle, who helped with our initial dam portages, plus my friends Jeff and Becky Blend who brought the trailer across Montana to help us portage around Fort Peck Dam. There we moved beyond my network of family and friends into the arms of River Angels

The badlands are rich in subtle hues and not so desolate as in Montana.

Trapped by a log.

A black seam of coal is visible in the cut bank.

The coal seam visible in the left bank long ago caught fire in the right bank, firing the badlands clay to red brick.

Wind-driven waves lap away at the lakshore, eroding rounded green hills into cliff-like cut banks.

Peg drove us to the "Birnt Hills" where Lewis was shot in the butt by one of his own men on their return trip in 1806.

who graciously help long distance paddlers. The first were Rod and Diane Gorder, who made a six-hour round-trip drive to deliver the canoe trailer to Tobacco Gardens Resort and Marina on Lake Sakakawea.

Another Angel came in the form of Charles Tatch, who drove up from Georgia to join the expedition at Trenton Lake. He'd read some of my books and followed the expedition with great interest. He asked if there was anything we needed. I couldn't think of anything at first. He asked again, so I offhandedly asked, "Would you happen to have a gas or electric outboard motor laying around...?"

Charles brought both, plus mounting hardware, gas cans, a battery charger and a big solar panel, dried fruit and nuts, fresh Georgia peaches, and more. We left the motors in his truck while paddling down the river and the first twenty grueling miles of Lake Sakakawea to Tobacco Gardens.

There we were greeted by proprietor Peg Hellandsaas who has a soft heart for the bedraggled paddlers who wash up on her beach. Tobacco Gardens is the make-it-or-break-it point for many paddlers, she explained. Slaying the Lakeness Monster at Fort Peck is totally achievable. It's the reward of taking on two more beasts back-to-back that overwhelms many paddlers, especially if they hit Sakakawea during stormy weather.

Much to our astonishment, Peg provided courtesy cabins, showers, and meals for the crew. More than a River Angel, she is known as River Mom. She catered to our every need or wish while we were there. Her crew drove Charles back upriver to get his truck and the outboard motors.

We clamped the 4-cycle Honda motor to the tail of Belladonna Beaver the dugout canoe and did a test run in the bay. It worked! The electric trolling motor went on Scott's Old Town canoe, which worked, although not nearly as powerful as the gas motor.

Peg drove us up to the Birnt Hills Overlook, where interpretive signs describe how Lewis was shot in the butt by a near-sighted crewman who mistook him for an elk on their 1806 return trip to St. Louis.

In the morning, we signed Peg's paddler guest book and wrote a note on her paddles. It was fun to read the notes of fellow paddlers who have preceded us over the years.

To keep the fleet together, we used driftwood and paracord to lash Scott's canoe to the dugout like an outrigger, then tied Charles's solo canoe on back for towing, manned by John. Scott named our new ship the *Contraption*. It was mid-afternoon by the time we launched, the worst time of day to be on the water.

We signed the paddles.

Rowdy caught a nice bass.

Peg gave us the royal treatment at Tobacco Gardens Resort and Marina.

Peg and I tested the motor on Belladonna Beaver.

133

The badlands feature warm colors and fertile grasslands, not really badlands at all!

Dotted gayfeather (Liatris punctata).

We motored into a headwind, the rolling waves funneling in between the two canoes and sloshing over the gunnels. With the motor doing the work, we traded paddles for sponges, attempting to keep up with the incoming waves. Scott and Chris improvised a dam between the canoes with a tarp and heavy dry bags, stopping most of the water. Charles and I discovered we could steer by ruddering with the paddles, rather than constantly adjusting the motor.

We sped along the lake at 1.8 mph, the fastest we could plow into a headwind without swamping the canoes. After an eternally long time at sea, we motored into a protective bay and pitched camp all of three air miles from our launch at Tobacco Gardens. The *Contraption* proved herself minimally sea-worthy under poor conditions. We could only do better from there, as long as we had Angels to guide us.

Charles and I manned the back of the Contraption.

"We [...] hoisted both the sails in the White Perogue, consisting of a small squar sail, and spritsail, which carried her at a pretty good gate, untill about 2 in the afternoon when a suddon squall of wind struck us and turned the perogue so much on the side as to allarm Sharbono who was steering at the time, in this state of alarm he threw the perogue with her side to the wind, when the spritsail gibing was as near overseting the perogue as it was possible to have missed. the wind however abating for an instant I ordered Drewyer to the helm and the sails be taken in, which was instant executed and the perogue being steered before the wind was agin plased in a state of security. this accedent was very near costing us dearly."

—Meriwether Lewis, April 13, 1805

Motoring into the morning sun with the Contraption.

Chronicles of the Contraption

Powerful east winds enabled Lewis and Clark to sail up parts of the Missouri River that now lie at the bottom of Lake Sakakawea. Winds we encountered were not as strong, yet still challenging for our canoe contraption. We bounced through the waves, bailing water out while the motor did all the work.

With optimal lake conditions, the *Contraption* maintained a steady 4.7 mph. It was a thrill to watch the scenery blow by at faster-than-walking speed. And with oil wells on shore, there was something oddly appropriate about motoring the lake burning petrol.

Although motorized, the *Contraption* retained the limitations of her component parts, necessitating protective harbors from wind and waves. The lashed poles bounced up and down like the whole thing was going to fly apart at any moment, and big waves threatened to fill the canoes. Taking shelter in a bay during one thundershower, we pitched our tents in a green, flat-bottomed wash, only to have the runoff fan out inches deep under our tents.

Photo by Scott Robinson

Flooded out of our tents.

135

Lake conditions were never particularly severe, however, and while we hunkered down for survival, people with real boats were cruising back and forth on the lake having a party. The short-lived storm brought out colors in the landscape, here dominated by brick-red hues of hills long ago fired by burning coal seams.

Lake Sakakawea is largely vacated during weekdays and incredibly beautiful. The surrounding terrain features badlands characteristics with soft earthy hues composed of more silt than clay, overlain with rich, fertile prairie. I anticipated hot, dry weather, but with the succession of storms we endured, the land was as green as spring.

A passing storm brought out colors in the landscape.

At Phelps Bay we stayed an extra day to allow turbulent weather to pass through. Charles made a bow and drill fire set and started his first-ever friction fire. We all took refuge in his oversize tent to play a game of Wildlife Web. Between storms the weather was nice enough to hike and explore the area. Mats of creeping juniper (*Juniperus horizontalis*) blanketed the hills like gigantic green carpets. I found anise-scented hyssop (*Agastache foeniculum*) to give a nice licorice flavor to my water bottle.

Peg at Tobacco Gardens had sent two big bags of gourmet beef short rib leftovers from her restaurant, providing several top-notch meals. For dinner I fried ribs with onions, sow thistle greens, and buffaloberries. The Missouri River Corps of Rediscovery ate well!

We enjoyed great hikes exploring around Phelps Bay.

Charles and puppy.

We blended Peg's beef short ribs with onions, south thistle greens and buffaloberries.

137

We motored Lake Sakakawea with John in tow.

Approaching Four Bears Bridge on the Fort Berthold Reservation.

Progress on Lake Sakakawea was slow due to the weather and excess caution when reading the weather forecasts, sometimes staying put when we could have traveled. We debated if it would be better to move forward at 1.5 mph in choppy waves to keep making progress or wait for calm conditions to speed along at 4.5+ mph. Fortunately, we enjoyed calm waters from Phelps Bay to Four Bears, covering fifteen miles in only a few hours.

Charles departed at Four Bears, bound for home in Georgia. He donated the outboard motor to the expedition along with the green Rogue River canoe he bought off Craigslist. We were sorry to see him go and hoped he might return for another section of the river. On the way, he shuttled the canoe trailer from Tobacco Gardens southeast to the Garrison Dam.

At the Four Bears earthlodge village, we met Darian Morsette, tourism director for the Mandan, Hidatsa, and Arikara (Sahnish) Nation, otherwise known as the Three Affiliated Tribes of Fort Berthold Reservation. Darian gave us the grand tour of the earthlodges and cultural center. The tribes speak different languages, but share much of their culture in common. All three were horticultural societies that grew great gardens featuring corn, beans, and squash. Known as the "three sisters," beans fix nitrogen in the soil for the corn, the corn provides a tall stalk for the beans, and big squash leaves help protect soil moisture and suppress weeds. All three tribes built earthlodges for shelter against cold and wind.

The three tribes previously lived separately, but grouped together for mutual defense in response to smallpox epidemics that decimated the population. Like other tribes, they signed treaties agreeing to reservation lands that were later unilaterally reduced by the U.S. Government, from 12 million acres to 8 million to 1 million acres. The final blow came in 1949 when the tribes were forced to cede 155,000 acres of fertile river valley, 94% of their farmland, for the construction of Garrison Dam

Fort Berthold is home to the Three Affiliated Tribes.

The tribes were forced to sign away their best land for Lake Sakakawea.

Jubilee encounters a cougar.

We camped in earthlodges for the night.

Gas flares light up the night sky.

Inside the main earthlodge and cultural center.

Darian gave us the grand tour.

Inside view of an earthlodge.

Petrified tree stump.

Wild raspberry.

and the creation of Lake Sakakawea. Residents were forcibly moved to exposed, windy plains, geographically separated from each other by the waters of the lake and its many big bays. Long-time assimilation programs forbade Native Americans from speaking their own languages, leading to extinction of the Mandan language and the near loss of Hidatsa and Sahnish.

The Three Affiliated Tribes are making the best of a difficult situation. While Darian lacked the opportunity to learn his native language, his son Kobe is learning Hidatsa in school. The Three Affiliated Tribes built the earthlodge village, host pow wows, and are working to preserve their cultural history. A major new cultural center is under construction.

I showed Darian pictures of an earthlodge I built for our wilderness survival programs back home. He invited us to camp overnight, and we moved into the cozy shelters moments before another storm rolled through.

Bur Oak (Quercus macrocarpa).

140

Favorable conditions allowed a full day of travel. Exploring a coulee during lunch, I found petrified tree stumps, apparently dawn redwoods (*Metasequoia*) from the 55 million-year-old Sentinel Butte Formation when the area was a coastal floodplain.

We covered thirty-eight miles for the day and camped by a bay near Independence Point, named after a town drowned under the lake. In a coulee near camp we explored a pocket of midwestern forest featuring oak, ash, box elder, aspen, willow, dogwood, wild plum, chokecherry, Virginia creeper, raspberry, and wild grapes. Poison ivy was abundant in patches and sometimes difficult to avoid. Jubilee ran through the thick of it, leaving me concerned that Chris might get a reaction from the oils on her fur, but fortunately, no harm done.

Motoring into moderate waves.

Virgin's Bower (Clematis virginiana).

Great scenery and pockets of midwestern forest surround Lake Sakakawea.

Some days I remember to brush my hair.

Cleaving bluffs make temporary blocky islands before all is eroded into the lake.

Binoculars are essential in the big open spaces.

The land flattens out near Beaver Creek.

Ripe buffaloberries.

I found a nice mess of meadow mushrooms.

Photo by Scott Robinson

Bow plow. Belladonna Beaver pushes through the water as we motor across the lake.

Placid conditions allowed us to putter thirty-three miles closer to the dam the following day. At camp I harvested giant horse mushrooms (*Agaricus arvensis*), which we fried for breakfast. I wish we could have explored every coulee along the lake, yet we saw traces of the first red and yellow fall colors. Snowberries were beginning to ripen, reminding us to keep moving as the Missouri has finally begun to swing south.

A strong tailwind pushed us forward, but blew so hard that John's tethered canoe rammed the back of the *Contraption* and knocked the motor off. We saved it, thanks to Scott's quick hands and redundant cords wrapped around critical components. We later remounted the motor and puttered into Dakota Waters Resort, welcomed by Amber Kimball who graciously offered a courtesy campsite.

The motorized Contraption was a huge aid in crossing the big lake.

The dogwoods are already showing fall colors.

Campers gifted us gourmet leftovers, here bacon-wrapped stuffed peppers.

Seeing John eat out of a tin can, our neighbors unloaded a pile of surplus barbecue buffalo wings, stuffed green peppers, baby baked potatoes, and roast beef which they would otherwise "toss in the dumpster." That was moments before we joined Amber, Thomas, and Christine for an amazing dinner of ribs, fresh corn, and baked potatoes.

I lost weight on the "All I Can Eat Diet Plan," but that may not last.

It may not look like much, but the excess water coming through the spillway greatly raises the river level.

Calm waters allowed us to reach Lake Sakakawea State Park the following day where we dismantled the *Contraption* back to her component canoes. We consumed five gallons of gas in 100 miles of lake travel.

River angel Nate McCleery and his father Mike, owners of the Sakakawea Sunset Lodge, helped us portage us around Garrison Dam. Portaging turned into a detour to the lodge for plush courtesy rooms, hot showers, and gourmet dining in their restaurant. We were floored by everyone's kindness and generosity.

Mike and friend Bob Willcuts helped us launch in the morning, and since Bob was driving south shortly, he offered to transport the trailer to the next dam and find a suitable place to park it. Paddling downstream, we all agreed that North Dakota is the most hospitable state in the nation!

We return to paddling on the river between the lakes.

"The Main Chief Big White & 2 others i e the Big Man or Sha-ha-ca and [blank] Came early to talk, and Spoke as follows, after Smoking, Viz... We were Sorry when we heard of your going up but now you are going down, we are glad, if we eat you Shall eat, if we Starve you must starve also."

—William Clark, November 1, 1804

Forts and Villages

With his words of welcome, Chief Sheheke invited the Corps of Discovery to winter near the Knife River Mandan villages, north of today's Bismarck, North Dakota. French traders dubbed the chief "Big White" due to his size and complexion. Without the friendship and hospitality of the Mandans and other tribes along the journey, it is doubtful that Lewis and Clark would have made it to the Pacific Ocean and back.

Our Missouri River Corps of Rediscovery has also benefited from the tradition of friendship and hospitality as we retrace their route and move backwards through their journals to 1804.

Stormy weather greeted our return to the free-flowing river. Grey clouds turned to dripping rain as we paddled downstream from Garrison Dam in search of Knife River Indian Villages National Historic Site. Lacking clear access from the Missouri, we docked our canoes at a boat ramp and walked down the road in the rain, not sure if it was public or private land. The landowner drove up moments later and rolled down his window. We explained our mission, and Bill Marlenee offered a ride, then told us about this guy he knew named Churchill Clark who carves dugout canoes. Such is the serendipitous nature of our journey that we would stumble into a friend of a friend nearly a thousand river miles from home.

We toured Knife River Indian Villages National Historic Site

Cozy home furnishings inside the earthlodge.

The "three sisters garden" includes corn, beans, and squash.

Dry corn, beans, and squash were stored in underground caches.

The Knife River site was settled around 1525. Lewis and Clark found two independent Mandan villages and three independent Hidatsa villages totaling up to 5,000 citizens. The Mandans and Hidatsa spoke different languages, but shared similar cultures and often lived near each other for mutual defense.

French Canadian trader Toussaint Charbonneau and his Shoshone-born teenage wife lived among the Hidatsa in Awatixa Village. Lewis and Clark hired him as an interpreter, bringing Sacagawea and her newborn son along as the newest and youngest members of the Corps of Discovery.

A reconstructed earthlodge at Knife River is outfitted with the furnishings of the day to provide an enchanting glimpse into life in an earthlodge village. Gardens feature the "three sisters" of corn, beans, and squash that complimented each other and provided the main staples of these horticultural tribes.

Bill drove us to nearby Fort Clark Trading Post State Historic Site, where interpretive signs mark grassy mounds of long-gone structures. The fort was built by the American Fur Company in 1830 beside another Mandan village. The steamboat St. Peters docked there in 1837 carrying passengers infected with smallpox. The subsequent epidemic killed at least 17,000 Indigenous people along the Missouri River, in some cases wiping out entire villages. The village was abandoned as

We bumped into Bill Marlenee, a friend of Churchill Clark.

Desk Doggy.

Leland Olds Station runs on lignite coal.

survivors joined the Knife River Villages, and all soon migrated north to form Like-a-Fishook Village, which now lies beneath Lake Sakakawea.

Bill and Debra Marlenee kindly invited our unexpected entourage to stay in their cabin, a greatly appreciated gesture on a cold, rainy night. Hot pizza for dinner and a hearty big breakfast of eggs, sausage, hash browns, and rolls didn't hurt either. How can we repay such kindness everywhere we go?

A solid day of paddling brought us to Washburn, where we found courtesy camping in the waterfront city park. Renewed hunger brought us to the Ice Burg for burgers, fries, and chocolate shakes, as if we have completely forgotten how to cook for ourselves.

Spending two nights and a day in town, we toured the Lewis and Clark Interpretive Center and the reconstructed Fort Mandan. Having built my own home, it is difficult to conceive how the Corps of Discovery managed to construct the substantial fort in a matter of weeks, let alone make it livable to survive severe winter weather with temperatures dropping to -45°F.

The original fort burned down before their return in 1806, and the river has since washed away the site, so the replica fort was constructed downstream. Our tour guide and interpreter, Shannon Kelly, remembered buying books from me at a Lewis and Clark event years ago as a teenager. She brought a pumpkin cake out to our camp in celebration of Lewis's 245th birthday on the 18th.

We found our way back to the Ice Burg numerous times, where we were served by Kirsten Olson. She gifted us her amazing homemade bacon and breakfast sausage for the trail.

Captains' quarters at the reconstructed Fort Mandan.

Life at Fort Mandan as depicted in a mural curated by the McClean County Historical Society at the county museum in Washburn.

I met Shannon Kelly at Fort Mandan.

Tools of the map maker.

Games and music provided entertainment.

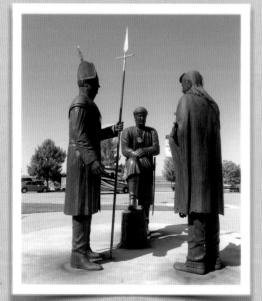

*Lewis and Clark confer with
Mandan Chief Sheheke at the
Lewis and Clark Interpretive Center*

Sunset as viewed from the city park in Washburn.

Seven miles later, we camped at Cross Ranch State Park to hike the extensive park trail system. Once owned by Teddy Roosevelt, the park retained the name based on his Maltese cross cattle brand. The Nature Conservancy bought most of the ranch and donated the riverfront to North Dakota for the park in 1989, while retaining the rest as the Cross Ranch Preserve. TNC raises 200 bison on the preserve. I hiked the public trail into the nature preserve to see the bison, but they were in another pasture at the time.

One huge "grandfather" cottonwood tree within the park was alive even before Lewis and Clark passed by. Wherever we went, we enjoyed snacking on ripe chokecherries, buffalo berries, and now wild grapes. I cooked a batch of wild grape syrup for our pancakes.

Scott paddled solo after John took over Charles' canoe.

Maximilian sunflower
(Helianthus maximiliani)

Sandbars are common on the Missouri, but most lie submerged under this year's high waters.

151

This "grandfather" cottonwood started growing
before Lewis and Clark passed by.

Prairie onion (Allium stellatum)

Riverbank grape (Vitis riparia)

We stopped at Double Ditch Indian Village State Historic Site, so named for defensive earthworks built around earthlodge communities featuring a wooden palisade surrounded by a dry moat to deter attackers. As the population declined, the ditch was reduced in size, leaving two visible defensive ditches. The site was abandoned after a smallpox epidemic decimated the population in 1781. Ground squirrels are now the primary inhabitants, dragging scraps of bone, pottery, and flint to the surface as they tunnel through old waste middens.

Preparing to get back on the water, we were approached by three guys on a pontoon boat, who shouted out, "Are you guys the Corps of Rediscovery?"

"Yeah, you found us," I replied, assuming they were tracking our progress online. But they had not heard of the expedition; it was just a lucky guess made in good humor. Shortly thereafter, we pitched our tents on the lawn at Clete Burbach and Lesley Oliver's riverfront home north of Bismarck, joining them and guests Bill and Alexander Renney from Montana for a big steak dinner with fresh corn, mashed potatoes, and a big green salad.

Clete drove us around Bismarck in the morning to catch up on errands. We hoped to get Jubilee into the vet for puppy shots, but no openings were available. However, Clete's neighbor happened to be a retired

We enjoyed a calm day on the river.

Sunflowers bloom on a sandbar.

Defensive ditches persist centuries later.

Bird tracks on the beach.

153

Clete and Bill greeted us on the river.

veterinarian. John gave Jubilee a courtesy distemper/parvo vaccination just before we piled back into the canoes. Chalk another one up to serendipity.

Paddling into an afternoon headwind gained us only four wet miles. We camped on a protected beach on a willowy island waiting for the wind to abate, technically still north of Bismarck.

Six miles in the morning brought us to the confluence with the Heart River at Fort Abraham Lincoln State Park. We camped for two nights as another storm front rolled through. Established as an infantry post named Fort McKeen, the fort was later renamed after Lincoln and expanded to include a calvary post, led by General George Custer before he marched his forces to their doom against the Sioux at the Little Bighorn Battlefield in Montana.

The park includes On-A-Slant Indian Village, established in the 1500s as the

Passing under the Interstate 94 bridge.

American bittersweet (Celastrus scandens)

Several infantry post blockhouses secured the hilltop.

Soldiers primarily died from freezing, drowning, and illness.

Custer's house at Ft. Abraham Lincoln.

Mess hall in the garrison.

Our tour guide.

Inside General Custer's opulent home on the prairie.

Pottery and earthlodges date back to 500 B.C. in North Dakota, this pot on display at the North Dakota Heritage Center & State Museum.

Diorama at On-A-Slant Village shows what the full village might have looked like.

On-A-Slant Indian Village was constructed on a sloping hillside over the Missouri River, part of today's Fort Abraham Lincoln State Park.

The ceremonial earth lodge exceeds ninety feet in diameter.

southernmost Mandan village and home to more than 1,000 people. The village was constructed on a gently sloping hillside, hence the name.

On-A-Slant was inhabited until the 1781 smallpox epidemic killed most of the population and the survivors migrated north to join the Hidatsa at the Knife River site for mutual defense against the Sioux. Reconstructed earthlodges provide another glimpse into the lives of these horticultural peoples. The main ceremonial lodge appears small outside, but is actually quite large inside.

Finally back on the river, we paddled to Sugarloaf Recreation Area. Glenn, the park manager, was super helpful in giving us a good campsite. His wife cooked up a big lasagna in anticipation of guests that didn't arrive, so they gifted it to us. We are surely the most spoiled group to ever paddle the Missouri River!

Sunflowers bloom in abundance at Sugarloaf.

Driftwood on the beach.

Water smartweed
(Persicaria amphibia, a.k.a. Polygonum amphibium)

"At 6 miles passed the mouth of La Bullet or Cannon Ball River on the L. Side about 140 yards Wide, and heads near the Black Mountains above the mouth of this River, in and at the foot of the Bluff, and in the water is a number of round Stones, resembling Shells and Cannon balls of Different Sises, and of excellent grit for Grindstons— the Bluff continus for about a mile, The water of this River is confined within 40 yards."

—William Clark, October 18, 1804

Aloha Oahe!

After a pleasant week paddling the Missouri River near Bismarck, North Dakota, we came face-to-face with Lake Oahe. While the name sounds Hawaiian, "Oahe" is actually a Sioux word meaning "a foundation" or "a place to stand on." Christian missionaries established the Oahe Indian Mission among the Lakota Sioux near Pierre, South Dakota in 1874. The mission was salvaged, moved, and later restored when Oahe Dam was constructed in the 1950s.

At 230 miles long, Oahe is considered one of the most hazardous lakes for small watercraft on the Missouri. Mostly less than two miles wide, it is easy to cross the lake, except for the risk of sudden, severe winds. Submerged trees reportedly bob up and down in subsurface currents, sometimes lurching unexpectedly up out of the water. And when the reservoir is drawn down in late summer, a person may slog through a hundred yards of mud to reach shore.

While I admire those who have the gall to battle wind and waves for three or more weeks to conquer the lake with paddles, that was not our mission. From the outset I envisioned our expedition like a car camping trip, touring national parks. We substituted canoes for cars and float down the river, stopping to see sites of

The land is small but the sky is big.

Caught in a passing storm.

natural or historical interest along the way. For Oahe, we lashed our canoes back together to reform the *Contraption* and fired up the outboard motor to traverse the lake.

The upstream end of the lake is shallow and typically a quagmire of sandbars that are difficult to navigate. However, with high water this year, GPS maps indicated we were boating right over sandbars, our path inhibited only by great patches of smartweed standing erect in the water. It was a floating flower garden with dark green leaves and spikes of little pink flowers. We could have paddled straight through with individual canoes, but the more cumbersome *Contraption* required zipping back and forth across the lake in search of open water.

Jubilee listens to her Pa.

159

A passing storm gave us a rainbow over Cannonball Bay.

With a windstorm moving in, we puttered into the mouth of the Cannonball River and found a nicely protected campsite within the bay. The "cannonballs" Clark referred to in the journals are sandstone concretions, formed almost like pearls as minerals build up in layers around a small nucleus. Most of the cannonballs are now hidden under the waters of the lake. Although harmless, the site has a charged history.

The Cannonball River marks the northern boundary of the Standing Rock Indian Reservation. It was here, immediately north of reservation lands, that Energy Transfer Partners (ETP) chose to route the 30-inch Dakota Access Pipeline under the Missouri River. The pipeline connects the Bakken oil fields we encountered in western North Dakota to oil ports in Illinois.

Members of the Standing Rock tribe gathered and protested the pipeline project, concerned that it might leak and contaminate the Missouri River. There were also charges of environmental racism, that ETP routed the pipeline by the reservation to avoid more politically-connected white settlements near Bismarck.

As the protest gained national and international attention, outsiders showed up in droves and "NO DAPL" became a symbol for the need to end our dependence on oil and take serious action to halt global

Black-eyed Susan
(Rudbeckia hirta)

Wild cucumber
(Echinocystis lobata)

Stiff sunflower
(Helianthus pauciflorus)

warming. However, the $3.78 billion pipeline was already 75% complete, and the end was a forgone conclusion. ETP started the project without all the necessary permits in hand, knowing that nobody could stop the project once started.

The United States functions as a corportocracy where corporations pay lawmakers to write laws, and law enforcement is required to enforce those laws. Under the influence of corporate lobbyists, lawmakers granted the power of eminent domain to ETP to route the for-profit pipeline through private lands with or without landowner consent.

With law enforcement enlisted to protect corporate interests, and out-of-state protestors agitating the situation, the focus of the protest shifted from pipeline to police, degenerating into a "he said, she said" confrontation, each side hurling accusations of misconduct at the other. I heard it all from friends on both sides of the political divide.

We took a layover day due to high winds on the lake, so I hiked up to the pipeline to get a boots-on-the-ground perspective. Like battlefields of the past, the site is eerily quiet except for the blustery wind. The pipeline route across the hills is visible primarily by the different hues of grass used to revegetate the land. A prairie dog town has re-asserted itself around the drill pad where the pipeline dives under Lake Oahe. Although pipelines are considered safer than rail transport for oil, the Dakota Access Pipeline has already leaked several times, thankfully not yet into the Missouri River.

In another matter, we haven't seen Josiah in weeks. He twice paddled ahead to work odd jobs in towns along the way, this last time missing the rendezvous point after Williston. He shuttled ahead to catch up with us at Bismarck, but ran into friends traveling east and ended up in Minnesota. The Corps of Rediscovery now consists of four men and a dog.

A revegetated strip reveals the path of the Dakota Access Pipeline.

Prairie dogs refurbished their mounds in the wake of pipeline construction. Here the pipeline dives under the Missouri River.

An artificial island supports a transmission line across the lake.

Black-eyed Susan
(Rudbeckia hirta)

South Dakota

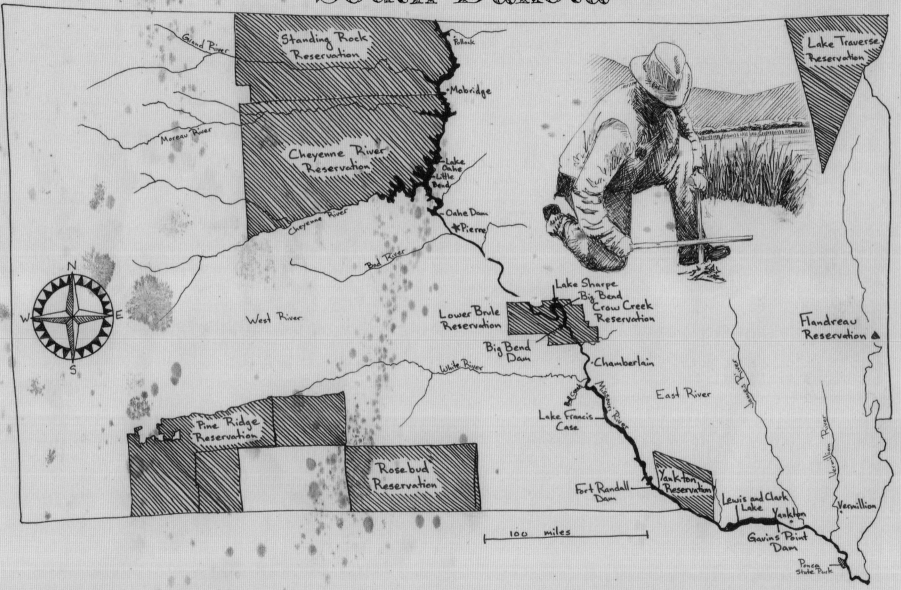

Grand River

Standing Rock Reservation

Pollock

Moreau River

Mobridge

Cheyenne River Reservation

Lake Traverse Reservation

Lake Oahe Little Bend

Cheyenne River

Oahe Dam

★ Pierre

Bad River

Lake Sharpe

Big Bend

Crow Creek Reservation

N W E S

West River

Lower Brule Reservation

Big Bend Dam

Chamberlain

Flandreau Reservation

White River

East River

James River

Lake Francis Case

Missouri River

Pine Ridge Reservation

Vermillion River

Rosebud Reservation

Lake Francis Case

Fort Randall Dam

Yankton Reservation

Lewis and Clark Lake

Yankton

Vermillion

100 miles

Gavins Point Dam

Ponca State Park

Prairie Rattlesnake (Crotalus viridis)

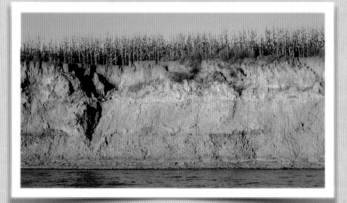

Corn is planted to the edge of the bank.

Jubilee loves every opportunity to run.

164

"Saw great numbers of goats or Antelope on Shore, Capt Lewis one man & the Ricara Chief walked on Shore, in the evening I discovered a number of Indians on each Side and goats in the river or Swiming & on Sand bars, when I came near Saw the boys in the water Swiming amongst the goats & Killing them with Sticks, and then hauling them to the Shore those on Shore Kept them in the water, I saw 58 Killed in this way and on the Shore, the hunter with Cap Lewis Shot 3 goats   I came too and Camped above the Ricara Camp on the L. S. Several Indians visited us duereing the night Some with meat, Sang and were merry all night."

—William Clark, October 16, 1804

The Hunted

Pronghorn, a.k.a. American antelope, or "goats" to Lewis and Clark, are the fastest land animals in North America, capable of running at speeds up to 55 mph in short bursts. Before firearms, people hunted with whatever weapons they could improvise with their own hands, aided by skill and a great deal of opportunistic good luck. The Sahnish people, better known as the Arikara—whom Lewis and Clark referred to as the Ricara, Stararee, Rickarree or Rees—herded pronghorn into pens where the animals could be slaughtered, or in the instance above, caught them crossing the river.

Like the pronghorn, we were also vulnerable in the water, our little ship bobbing around in the waves of the lake that drowned the river. We were the hunted, living a game of cat and mouse with the wind, scurrying from one protective cove to another when the wind was momentarily absent. We boldly bolted across the open lake when the wind slept.

The grassy prairie hills remained unseasonably green, the flatter portions plowed into corn fields that extended to the water's edge. Corn-fattened deer actively grazed in the evening light. I took several shots with my camera, but without a proper zoom, the shots went wide, and the deer escaped unscathed.

John paddled solo after the tether broke.

We camped on the sandy beach at State Line Resort one night, then lingered half the next day hoping for a break in the wind. Finally we puttered across the border from North to South Dakota, trying to outrun the wind on our tail. We could handle the breeze where the lake was narrow and the waves small, but the open waters of Pollack Bay magnified the swells higher than any we had encountered. Yet, these were surprisingly gentle big waves, and our principal challenge was the forward and back lurch of John's canoe in tow.

John progressively tied his canoe closer and closer to the *Contraption* to reduce the tail wag effect, yet the wind and waves still sent him lurching into the back of our ship. Scott moved the line to the outside of his canoe to protect the outboard motor, but the swells provided enough lurching momentum to repeatedly snap the 550-lb. rated paracord. After several failed tries, plus a loop back to retrieve a lost paddle, we finally motored ahead to a protected bay to wait while John paddled to catch up.

Fossil baculites littered the lake shore, plus I found a small squid fossil and the imprint of a large clam, all snapshots of an even more watery world from 135 million years ago. We finally got our break when the wind settled down in the evening, and we made a run for our next campsite, setting up tents just before darkness.

Another day on the water brought us to Mobridge where we met up with Scott's girlfriend Margie, who flew in from Colorado for the weekend. With the aid of Margie's

At a rest stop I found fossil baculite, squid, and a clam.

Bridges grow bigger and bigger, here the Highway 12 bridge at Mobridge, South Dakota, the town originally named after a railroad bridge.

165

Sacajawea, Sacagawea, or in the Dakotas, Sakakawea.

We visited the Sitting Bull Monument on the Standing Rock Reservation.

*Goldenrod
(Solidago gigantea)*

*Margie flew in from Colorado to
visit for the weekend.*

Photo by Scott Robinson

rental car, we toured the Sitting Bull and Sakakawea monuments, the Klein Museum, and the local cuisine. A country drive took us through corn fields, sunflowers, and a few bean fields, all traditional crops previously grown by the Hidatsa, Mandan, and Arikara tribes. The tribes stored thousands of bushels of food in underground caches.

Deborah Barnes from the Chamber of Commerce was super helpful to find us a campsite on a busy weekend at The Bay on the Standing Rock Reservation. She volunteered her husband Dana to wave us in to shore. She even brought her scissors to camp and gave John a haircut while Chris and I borrowed her electric shears to trim our beards.

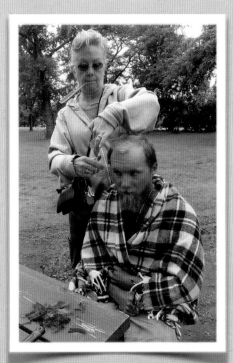

Deborah cut John's hair.

Margie enjoyed an evening on the bay with Scott.

Sunflowers were traditionally grown by native tribes, the plants now bred larger and cultivated as a major crop.

167

Pollinators love sunflower fields.

Every day brings a new campsite, a temporary home for our mobile tribe.

The total Arikara population numbered between 10,000 and 30,000 people before smallpox decimated their numbers. Survivors migrated north to live near the Mandan and Hidatsa villages for mutual defense. Lewis and Clark estimated there were 3,000 Arikara at the Knife River Villages in 1804.

Nomadic Sioux tribes suffered smaller losses to early smallpox epidemics, expanding to become the dominant culture of the northern plains. The Fort Laramie Treaty of 1851 outlined approximate territorial boundaries of western tribes, while the Treaty of 1868 defined the Great Sioux Reservation as encompassing all of South Dakota west of the Missouri River, with small extensions east of the river and south into present-day Nebraska.

In 1874, General George Custer and the 7th Cavalry entered the Black Hills in violation of the treaty, starting the gold rush and an invasion of white prospectors and settlers. The incursion ignited hostilities with the Sioux, leading to Custer's death at the Battle of the Little Bighorn in Montana just two years later. The U.S. government responded with the unilateral "Agreement of 1877," which halted treaty rations to the Sioux until they seized hostilities and ceded the Black Hills to the United States. The Great Sioux Reservation was split into five smaller reservations, including Standing Rock and the adjacent Cheyenne River Reservation.

Baby garter snake.

Evening primrose.

Morning dew glistens on a sulphur butterfly.

Fishermen at Lebeau Recreation Area said we were the first people they've encountered there in twenty years.

169

South Dakota / September 4 / Lake Oahe / Lebeau to Cow Bay

Our attempt to continue south from Mobridge was stymied by the wind stalking the lake. We learned to monitor hour-by-hour forecasts to seize opportunities as they arise. With late afternoon winds projected to switch from southeast to northwest, we slipped though the gap and covered fifteen miles in four hours, salvaging the day. We camped very near the halfway point of the Missouri River, approximately 1,170 miles upstream to the headwaters at Three Forks, Montana, or downstream to the river's confluence with the Mississippi.

Moving south, the land becomes softer, the grassy hills more rounded and tree cover largely absent. This is what we imagined the Dakotas would look like, albeit, not so green. A morning start was cut short when the cat blew by, sending us scurrying for a protective bay. With no shade and nowhere to go, we hung out in the sun and wind all day waiting for a break, gaining a few more miles in the evening.

An outboard motor should make the journey easy, but we only gained 3.5 miles the next day, windbound until night. Finally we got a calm day and made a run for it. Ten miles later the propeller stopped turning.

Paddling to shore, we neophytes disassembled the propeller and noticed the broken pin that connects the propeller to the shaft. We rummaged through our gear for a reasonable substitute. The wire handle on my stainless steel Zebra pot exactly matched the diameter. In less than an hour we completed our redneck repair. We were still congratulating ourselves on our resourcefulness when John pointed out two spare pins conveniently attached to the bottom of the motor. We covered eighteen more miles, arriving at Sutton Bay early enough to enjoy a relaxing evening.

John cooked lunch.

We saw surprisingly few cattle on our journey, more here than elsewhere, but on average perhaps one cow per mile over 1,170 miles.

*Velvetleaf
(Abutilon theophrasti)*

We saw fifteen pronghorn in the prairie hills, making a total of thirty since we left home 1,200 miles ago, paddling through some of the richest wildlife habitat in North America.

It is believed there were once 40 million pronghorn in the West, plummeting to 20,000 by 1900. Today the population has rebounded to an estimated 85,000 pronghorn, or 2.5% of their original numbers. Reading the journals of Lewis and Clark and the massive herds they encountered, I cannot help feeling that all the animals were somehow vacuumed up, like so many bugs in a rug.

Strangely, we saw one lone bison by the lakeshore, almost like a ghost animal. Does it belong to a public or private herd? Up to 60 million bison once roamed the continent. Only 325 animals survived the great culling. Today there are an estimated 200,000 bison, or 0.33% of their former numbers. One would imagine they were replaced by cattle, yet we've seen surprisingly few, perhaps one cow per mile of river on average, and many grassland pastures visibly ungrazed for many years.

With one day of good weather, followed by a forecast for wind and rain, we raced for Oahe Dam at 4 miles per hour and covered 40 miles in one long day to Sully Creek. We then took a layover day in a sheltered bay to wait out the storm.

*Turkey vulture
(Cathartes aura)*

Motoring across the big lake.

We improvised a replacement shear pin from my pot handle.

Sunflowers light up the evening sky.

Light filtering through the clouds created unusual blue streaks in the sky.

Barnyardgrass (Echinochloa sp.)

Wind-driven lake waves deposit debris across shallow bays, forming dams to create inland ponds and wetlands.

Snow-on-the-mountain flowers.

Gayfeather flowers (Liatris sp.)

Snow-on-the-mountain (Euphorbia marginata)

Bigroot prickly pear (Opuntia macrorhiza) produces edible, tasty fruits without spines.

We made fry bread and pasta for dinner.

South Dakota / September 8 / Lake Oahe / Sully Creek to Oahe Dam

Despite the blustery weather, we found ample time to explore and botanize along Sully Creek. I enjoyed the sweet red fruits of bigroot prickly pear, which are not covered with spines like the prickly pear cacti back home.

Our final day of Lake Oahe consisted of grey skies, temperatures in the mid-50s, blustery winds, and waves lapping over the sides of the canoes. We finished the lake damp and chilled, immensely grateful for help from Jesse Roebuck of the U.S. Army Corps of Engineers, who took time out of his Sunday to trailer us around Oahe Dam to camp at Oahe Downstream State Recreation Area.

I disturbed a few birds while paddling from the boat ramp to camp below the dam at Oahe Downstream State Recreation Area.

"The head chief the Black Buffaloe, Seized hold of the cable of the pearogue and Set down. Capt. Clark Spoke to all the party to Stand to their arms   Capt. Lewis who was on board ordered every man to his arms.   the large Swivel loaded immediately with 16 Musquet Ball in it   the 2 other Swivels loaded well with Buck Shot, Each of them manned. Capt. Clark used moderation with them told them that we must and would go on and would go.   that we were not Squaws, but warriers.   the chief Sayed he had warriers too and if we were to go on they would follow us and kill and take the whole of us by degrees or that he had another party or lodge above this and that they were able to destroy us."

—*Sargent John Ordway, September 25, 1804*

The Good River Encounter

The Missouri River bisects South Dakota as it flows south across the state. Known to South Dakotans as East River and West River, the wetter, more fertile eastern part of the state supports extensive croplands, while the larger western part features open prairie dominated by ranching and dryland farming. The two unequal halves are connected by six bridges with three additional roads crossing over dams. From our perspective, progressing from Lake Oahe to Lake Sharpe, the Missouri isn't so much a river, but a Great Moat ruled by tempestuous winds.

The state capitol is Pierre, a quaint small town with a population of 14,000. The town sits on east side a few miles downriver from Oahe Dam, near the geographical center of the state. This central location helped bring voters to the polls to out-compete larger towns for the capitol designation when South Dakota joined the Union in 1889.

With little wood available on the Great Plains, settlers used what resources were available, making sod homes from the prairie itself. Exhibit at the State Historical Society Museum.

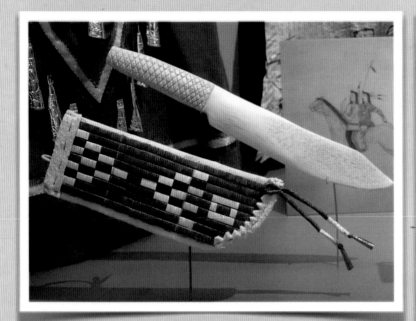

Bone knife and quilled sheath at the state museum.

River Cities Public Transit shuttled us from our campsite into town for a nominal fee on a pre-scheduled pick up. We enjoyed visiting the State Historical Society Museum, touring the town, and shopping for books and groceries. I bought a new spark plug for the outboard motor.

Mulberry trees in town and a sycamore tree at the campground, plus unfamiliar new bird calls, were all welcome signs that we were indeed migrating southward, albeit at a turtle's pace.

John solo paddled ahead in the morning, while Scott, Chris, and I paddled just six miles to Fischers Lilly Park at the Missouri's confluence with the Bad River in Fort Pierre, on the west side

Moonlight lights up the Missouri River and our canoes.

of the Missouri. This was the site of the Lewis and Clark Expedition's "Bad River Encounter" with the Teton Sioux or Lakota that nearly brought an early end to the Corps of Discovery. Clark and the chiefs managed to defuse the bad situation without violence. The standoff, however, was not the source of the name "Bad River." The Lakota previously named the river after a flash flood wiped out an Indian village.

For us it was the good river encounter because we met Caleb Gilkerson, captain of *The Sunset*, a diesel powered sternwheeler and the only authentic paddlewheel boat still operating on the Missouri River. Caleb was prepping the boat for an evening float, but invited us aboard for a tour and sodas.

Originally named *The Spirit of Cincinnati*, the boat was built in 1964, but in terrible shape when Caleb bought it in 2016. Piloting the vessel down the Ohio and up the Mississippi and Missouri rivers turned into a six-month ordeal of endless repairs. Thirty thousand people followed the journey on Facebook. Caleb noted that his posts were few and far between, as he didn't often have good news to report. Sometimes the ship drifted miles backwards when the engines failed and they couldn't stop the boat. Finally reaching Gavins Point Dam, he had to cut the top off the boat to portage it the remaining distance via highway to Pierre and Lake Sharpe. With a great deal of TLC, Caleb refurbished the boat, renamed it The Sunset, and now plies Lake Sharpe with guests and parties. With yet another storm brewing, we lashed the canoes back

We toured The Sunset, the only functional paddlewheel boat still operating on the Missouri.

Plant identification practice.

Wild cucumber (Echinocystis lobata)

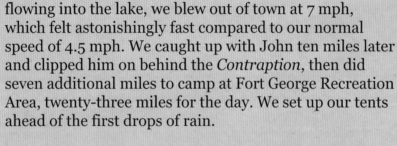

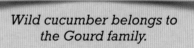

Photo by Scott Robinson

Wild cucumber belongs to
the Gourd family.

together and fired up the outboard motor for Lake Sharpe. Thanks to the river current flowing into the lake, we blew out of town at 7 mph, which felt astonishingly fast compared to our normal speed of 4.5 mph. We caught up with John ten miles later and clipped him on behind the *Contraption*, then did seven additional miles to camp at Fort George Recreation Area, twenty-three miles for the day. We set up our tents ahead of the first drops of rain.

Despite the motorized advantage, our lives remained dictated by the wind. We advanced only six miles the next day, thwarted by monster waves that loomed over our little ship. Like many places we camped, DeGrey Recreation Area was posted "No Camping," yet there seems to be a general exception for canoeists, since it would be unsafe to send us back onto the roiling waters.

It rained two inches overnight. Chris and Jubilee were flooded out of their tent within minutes and moved into mine. We took a layover day while the storm blew itself out. Hanging out provided a good opportunity for a botany walk. The guys recognized small flowered gaura as a member of the Evening Primrose family by its four-parted stigma. They were greatly improving in their plant identification skills!

Buffalo burr
(Solanum rostratum)

178

Harvesting Russian olive fruits.

Fungi sprout from a dead tree.

A monarch butterfly rests on a wild sunflower.

Russian olive fruits
(Elaeagnus angustifolia)

Cooking fry bread.

Migrating monarch butterflies rested at DeGrey Recreation Area.

Amorpha borer (Megacyllene decora)

Wild plums were planted in the shelter belt at DeGrey.

Tasting the Russian olives, I noted that the slightly yellow fruits were much sweeter than the grey, astringent ones in Montana. Squeezing the pit out of each one as I picked, I filled a 20-ounce bottle with processed fruits in 1 1/2 hours, then made fry bread consisting of Russian olives, wild plums, and flour. Not bad, but I think I could cook something more exciting.

Extensive windbreaks planted as "State Game Production Areas" help replace forest habitat drowned under the artificial lake, here featuring ash trees, chokecherries, wild plums, bur oak, junipers, honey locust, and lilacs. We were delighted to find thousands of monarch butterflies on their great migration back to central Mexico.

We continued our own migration when the weather finally broke, taking two days to navigate around the Big Bend of the Missouri, where the river takes a 25-mile loop before nearly coming back upon itself. William Clark walked over the narrow neck, noting the shortcut was about 1 1/4 miles across.

Photo by Scott Robinson

Chris and I steered as necessary with paddles from the stern.

Drowned trees in Lake Sharpe provide bird nesting habitat.

Monarch butterflies passed overhead in ones and twos. It's hard to believe any creature so small and delicate could migrate so far, even against ceaseless prairie winds, yet they were moving far faster than we were. They would complete their journey to Mexico in November while we were merely aiming for St. Louis.

In another good river encounter, Mike and Terri Mehlhaff and son Johnny of Pierre very kindly drove the canoe trailer from Oahe Dam to Good Soldier Creek Recreation Area to help us portage around Big Bend Dam, one more major hurdle out of the way!

Moonrise above Lake Sharpe as seen from West Bend State Recreation Area.

Photo by Scott Robinson

Seagulls fly ahead of us as Scott makes lunch on the water.

John rides along in tow. Motoring across the lakes is admittedly tedious for all of us!

We arrive at our portage point, ready to dismantle the Contraption… again.

"This morning set out at an early hour, and come too at ½ after 7 A. M. on the Lard. Shore 1¼ miles above the mouth of a small creek which we named Corvus, in consequence of having kiled a beatiful bird of that genus near it we concluded to ly by at this place the ballance of this day and the next, in order to dry our baggage which was wet by the heavy showers of rain which had fallen within the last three days, and also to lighten the boat by transfering a part of her lading to the red perogue, which we now determined to take on with us to our winter residence wherever that might be; while some of the men were imployed in this necessary labour others were dressing of skins washing and mending their cloaths &c."

—Meriwether Lewis, September 16, 1804

Big Bend Dam releases water to Lake Francis Case.

Layover

The waters of Lake Francis Case back up to the boat launch below Big Bend Dam and Lake Sharpe, so there is no free-flowing river between the two lakes. Having dismantled the *Contraption* to portage the canoes, we now lashed it back together to tackle this next section of the Great Moat across South Dakota. There were a dozen bystanders waiting to see us launch by the time we finished tying all the knots. We enjoyed an easy eighteen-mile day down to Chamberlain, where we took a layover day to tour the town.

A pelican comes in for a landing.

Pelicans are attracted to the tailwaters of the dam for fishing.

We toured the Akta Lakota Museum.

Indian breadroot was harvested, peeled, braided, and dried for storage. Outside, a horse and tipi.

Chamberlain is home to St. Joseph's Indian School, established as a boarding school in 1927. Like most such institutions of that time, St. Joseph's was founded on the ideology that it was necessary to suppress native language and culture to "help" their indigenous students assimilate into western culture. Children were punished for acts such as speaking Lakota in school.

Times have changed, and St. Joseph's has too. It is a residential-style school where children live in small family-sized groups in well-kept apartments. Native language and culture are included as part of the daily curriculum, bringing dignity back to the Lakota people. Parents can enroll their students in the school

Diorama shows tribal life on the Plains and an Indian woman tanning a bison hide.

184

at no cost, providing opportunities they may not have in their hometowns.

St. Joseph's hasn't been without controversy, but it is clearly appreciated by families of the two hundred children enrolled there. We toured the Akta Lakota Museum and Cultural Center at the school, which was exceptionally well done for a small museum.

It was also thrilling to see the Dignity sculpture at the rest area by the interstate highway. *Dignity of Earth and Sky* is a fifty-foot-tall stainless steel sculpture of an indigenous woman in Plains-style dress with her arms outstretched, receiving a star quilt. Dignity seems to welcome travelers, as if to embrace all who come to South Dakota.

From the American Creek Campground, it was a 2.5-mile hike up to the sculpture, or 4 miles by my original route in the dark without a map, taking a "short-cut" through the grassy hills and junipers. I knew the general direction as I pushed through chest-high weeds, back-tracked around swamps, stepped over minor crevasses to scale an old slumped hillside, skirted around the cemetery, and finally dashed across the interstate and climbed the grassy hill past the warning sign about poisonous snakes. I made the special trip to see the sculpture lit up at night, then returned by day with Scott to see it again and to tour the Lewis and Clark Interpretive Center.

Dignity of Earth and Sky isn't a specific woman, but a composite of three different South Dakotan models honoring the Lakota and Dakota people of the state. It was created by South Dakota artist laureate Dale Claude Lamphere and funded by Norm and Eunabel McKie of Rapid City.

"Standing at a crossroads, Dignity echoes the interaction of earth, sky, and people. She brings to light the beauty and promise of indigenous peoples and cultures that still thrive on this land."

185

Lewis and Clark brought axes and pipe tomahawks for trade.

I am glad to see the Lakota and Dakota peoples honored after two centuries of oppression and cultural suppression. I hope that coming generations grow up with a sense of pride and dignity in being Native American.

Our tour of the interpretive center on September 16th coincided with Lewis and Clark's arrival on the same date, narrowly missing them by just 215 years. They camped on the opposite side of the Missouri near the present day town of Oacoma, taking a layover day to dry and repack their gear.

We were doing basically the same thing, drying wet gear, resupplying and organizing our food supplies, doing laundry, and hiking about the countryside. We

Photo by Scott Robinson

We foraged ripe mulberries in Chamberlain.

Standing on the dock.

ultimately took an additional layover day due to windy conditions on the lake. Where Lewis and Clark went out hunting big game, I hiked nearly four miles out to the I-90 interchange hunting for an ice cream cone, then hitch-hiked a ride back to camp, having walked more than twenty miles during our short stay in this pleasant small town.

Mosasaurs stalked the inland sea eighty million years ago; fossils have been found near Chamberlain.

On the 18th, Lewis and Clark proceeded northward on their Journey of Discovery, while we proceeded southward on our Journey of Rediscovery. We made it out of camp before sunrise, trusting the weather report that the winds would abate. I piloted the *Contraption* while Chris rode shotgun, or rather bail bucket, continuously bailing water for an hour until the wind and waves finally settled.

Passing below the Interstate 90 bridge seemed a noteworthy milestone. The last time we saw I-90 was four miles upriver from our initial launch point at Missouri Headwaters State Park near Three Forks, Montana. After three and a half months traveling north, east, and finally south, it is reassuring to see that we are making measurable progress in our attempt to migrate ahead of the changing seasons.

"*George Shannon who had been absent with the horses 16 days joined the boat about one oclock. he informed us that the reason of his keeping on so long was that he see some tracks which must have been Indians. he to[ok] it to [be] us and kept on, his bullets he Shot all away & he was with out any thing to eat for about 12 days except a fiew Grapes, he had left one of the horses behind, as he Gave out, only one horse with him he had gave up the idea of finding our boat & was returning down the river in hopes to meet Some other Boat, he was near killing the horse to Satisfy hunger, &C. &.C— he Shot a rabit with Sticks which he cut & put in his gun after his Balls were gone.*"

—*Sargent John Ordway, September 11, 1804*

We proceeded onward.

Sour Grapes

Of the three big lakes that comprise the Great Moat across South Dakota, Oahe, Sharpe, and Francis Case, Lake Francis Case is the most scenic. The surrounding terrain is more hilly, and in places angular, rugged, and much of the lake perimeter is richly forested. Like all of the artificial lakes, waves lapping at the shore undermine the hills until they cleave off into the water. Before and after Chamberlain, these cleaved faces resemble limestone cliffs, but consist largely of dense shale.

Much of Lake Francis Case is lined with scenic cliffs of bentonite-rich Pierre shale (75-81 mya) overtop the Niobrara Formation (82-87 mya).

Pelicans fly south for the winter. We would later encounter them again in Missouri.

Morning sunlight reflects off trees onto the placid waters of Lake Francis Case.

Woody debris is common in parts of Lake Francis Case.

Jubilee sleeps the day away on the long boat rides.

Ten miles downstream from Chamberlain, the aptly named White River enters the reservoir from the west, its chalky-muddy waters briefly restoring the "Big Muddy" character to the Missouri, readily visible even on Google Earth. But soon the sediments settle out in the lake, and the water regains its semi-transparent greenish hue.

Bull Creek enters the lake a mile farther down on the same side. Originally named Shannon Creek by Meriwether Lewis, George Shannon stayed there for several days subsisting on nothing but wild grapes.

On August 26, 1804, Shannon and George Drouillard hiked overland in search of the Expedition's missing horses. Drouillard came back the following morning after walking all night. He hadn't seen Shannon or the horses. John Shields and Joseph Field went after Shannon and found his tracks headed upstream, but couldn't catch up with him. Shannon was moving upriver desperately trying to catch up the Expedition that was still behind him. Getting separated from the group is a tricky problem. How do you determine if the boats are upstream or downstream?

Shannon was eighteen years old, the youngest man on the expedition, and a bit of a greenhorn. Although he recently killed an elk for the Corps of Discovery, Clark wrote, *"This man not being a first rate Hunter, we deturmined to Send one man in pursute of him with Some Provisions."* John Colter returned a couple days later and hadn't been able to catch up with him either.

Shannon shot away all the lead balls for his muzzleloader, then resorted to carving wooden bullets to kill a rabbit. He otherwise subsisted on sour wild grapes for most of his escapade. He finally gave up the chase and waited by the riverbank in hopes of meeting a boat traveling downstream, giving the Expedition a chance to catch up with him from behind.

While the original Corps of Discovery moved upstream, our goal was to migrate downstream ahead of fall weather. Even with the outboard motor, we consumed six weeks navigating all the lakes of the Dakotas. We became focused on the end goal, seeking the shortest route from point to point without taking time to explore side bays or truly appreciate the scenery.

Scott and I took turns at the helm. On my days off, I sat upfront to read books, write, nap, or practice the harmonica, re-assured that the drone of the motor was loud enough to drown out my tedious lessons. With a brief lull in the wind and waves, we made a run for the dam and almost made it. High winds forced another layover day fifteen miles from the end.

As a wilderness survival instructor, I've often wondered how I would have fared in George Shannon's situation. If need be, I could provide for most of my needs in a survival situation with a knife or without one. I've built and slept in warm shelters without blankets or a sleeping bag. I know how to start a fire by rubbing sticks together, and I know most of the edible plants in the U.S.

Like Shannon, however, my hunting skills could be better. I've successfully hunted rabbits, squirrcls, and grouse with sticks and rocks, and sometimes they are patient enough to allow multiple throws. I've used wooden spears and deadfall traps for porcupines, muskrats, and ground squirrels. I know how to catch fish with my hands or make a fish hook from thorns and line from plant fibers.

High winds and big waves necessitated a layover day.

Crown vetch (Securigera varia)

Rubbing foxtail millet seeds from the chaff.

Foxtail millet harvest.

Virginia groundcherry (Physalis virginiana)

Yet, I am primarily an opportunistic hunter, which requires the luck of being in the right place at the right time.

Shannon had a muzzleloader rifle, which could be used to shoot game and start a fire. He also likely had a knife, but anything beyond that is conjectural. He would have been fine if he could shoot game, drink out of the river, and sleep by a fire. In comparison, I have no experience with a muzzleloader, leaving me more dependent on wild food foraging.

Taking a layover day to explore lands similar to those Shannon roamed, we found additional wild edible plants beyond sour grapes. Hackberry fruits are edible and tasty, just not very fleshy. Crunch through the shell to eat the small nutmeat for protein and oils. Wild sunflower seeds are small, but highly nutritious, and they were grown as a crop by the Mandans. Cattails rhizomes are rich in carbohydrate starches. There are also a great many crickets and grasshoppers which are totally edible.

Grass seeds are also edible, although not always readily processable, and many new species have been introduced after Shannon's time. I harvested foxtail millet seeds, which I added to fry bread. Considering the possibilities, I might have eaten more, yet been just as hungry for meat as George Shannon.

One of his best sources of sustenance was the horse, which he considered killing. Optionally, he could have tapped a vein and drank enough blood each day to stay well-nourished without killing the horse.

They say hindsight is 20/20, and I'm sure Shannon later learned many tricks that would have helped him survive more comfortably. His skills at age eighteen were no doubt better than mine at the same age. Moreover, Shannon never spent a teenage day lazing on the couch watching television or playing video games. He likely learned to work hard and endure

We launched early, blessed with a breath-taking sunrise for our final day on Lake Francis Case.

difficult situations long before his survival ordeal. In a survival situation, shear will to keep going is perhaps the most important skill of all.

When the wind finally settled down, we arose before dawn and made the final push to Fort Randall Dam, thrilled to be finished with all the big lakes and relieved to be done with the outboard motor.

Fort Randall Dam holds back the waters of Lake Francis Case.

Tom Muenster portaged us around the dam.

Catclaw sensitive briar
(Mimosa nuttallii)

Soldiers at Fort Randall cut chalkstone with saws to build the chapel in 1875.

We continued downriver below the dam.

Chalkstone bluffs line the Missouri below Fort Randall.

Nebraska - Iowa

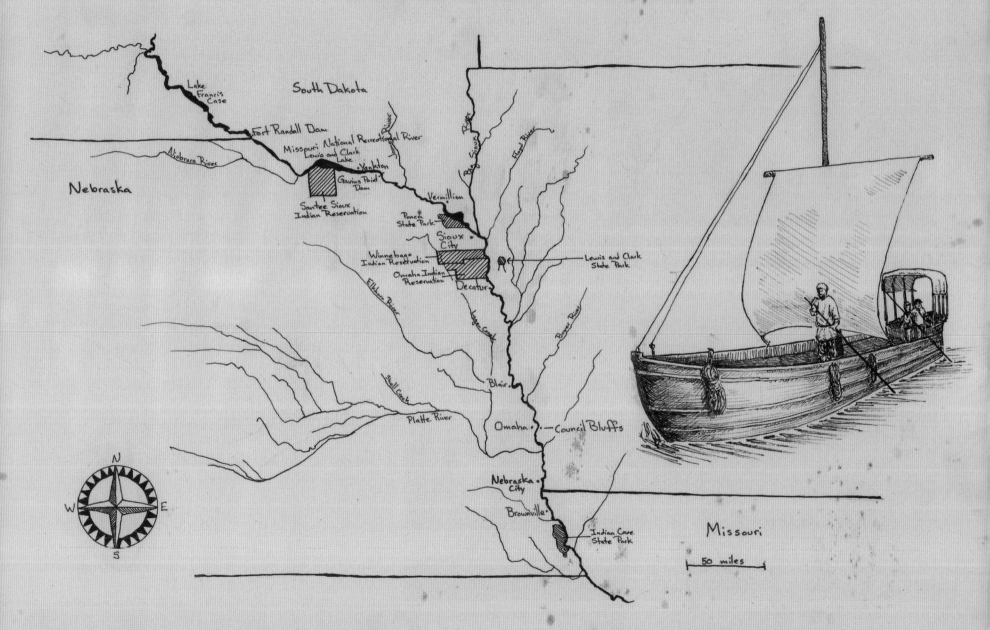

South Dakota

Lake Francis Case

Nebraska

Niobrara River

Fort Randall Dam

Missouri National Recreational River
Lewis and Clark Lake

Yankton

Gavins Point Dam

Santee Sioux Indian Reservation

Vermillion

Ponca State Park

Sioux City

Winnebago Indian Reservation

Lewis and Clark State Park

Omaha Indian Reservation

Decatur

Elkhorn River

Logan Creek

Boyer River

Shell Creek

Blair

Platte River

Omaha • — Council Bluffs

Nebraska City

Brownville

Indian Cave State Park

Missouri

50 miles

N
W   E
S

John caught a nice bass.

"Passed the mouth of the River Que Courre (rapid R[)] on the L. S. and Came to a Short distance above, this River is 152 yards wide at the mouth & 4 feet Deep Throwing out Sands like the Platt (only Corser) forming bars in its mouth, I went up this river three miles to a butifull Plain on the upper Side where the Panias once had a Village   this river widens above its mouth and is devided by Sand and Islands, the Current verry rapid, not navagable for even Canoos without Great dificulty owing to its Sands."

—William Clark, September 4, 1804

Throwing Sand

Fort Randall Dam marks the end of the Great Moat across South Dakota, just a few miles shy of the Nebraska border. The canoe trailer beat us there, thanks to Cliff Jager, who watched our last launch and offered to drive the trailer downriver. We were then helped by Tom Muenster, whom we first met at Gates of the Mountains back in Montana. He was leading a two-week expedition by pontoon boat, exploring segments of the upper Missouri portion of the Lewis and Clark National Historic Trail. Tom graciously volunteered to help us with the portage around the dam. We afterwards sent the outboard motor home with him for storage, thrilled at the prospect of paddling free-flowing water!

This point marks the start of the upper portion of the Missouri National Recreational River, one of the few river segments outside Montana still more-or-less unchanged from the days of Lewis and Clark. Here the Missouri flows southeast, marking the border between South Dakota and Nebraska. The

It's nice to be back to paddling after six weeks of motoring lakes across the Dakotas.

The Missouri National Recreational River hasn't been significantly altered like the rest of the lower Missouri River.

MNRR is administered by the National Park Service in cooperation with the two states. Flowing with the river current, it was satisfying to be propelled without a propellor.

Warm hues of orange-tinged chalky limestone bluffs lined the river, topped by cedar woodlands intermixed with a smattering of green ash, burr oak, and Russian olive. We enjoyed a relaxing float down to Sunshine Bottoms Landing on the Nebraska side. Feeling like a great explorer, this was the first time I set foot in the state. Nebraska always seemed so distant from my Montana home, yet it took us less than four months to get here!

Hemp is wild and abundant here.

The Missouri keeps growing wider the farther downriver we travel.

John paddled through flooded yards at Verdel.

Field corn grew on one side of the access road and beans on the other. Weeds filled in neglected gaps along the roadside and fence lines, including weed itself. We first noted a feral patch of pot back on Lake Sharpe, which then became a common sight along Lake Francis Case. This far south, marijuana was abundant and fully integrated into the ecosystem.

Would the Corps of Discovery have smoked pot if it grew here two centuries ago? Probably, given their lust for alcohol and tobacco, which were hauled across the continent and metered out to the crew as rewards along the way. However, we theorized that this plant was probably hemp, a variety of *Cannabis* useful for its fibers more than for any psychoactive properties.

The Missouri River was much as I imagined it, big and full of water. Yet, this year was unlike any known prior year. Lewis and Clark traveled upstream against a shallow, braided river, struggling to find deep enough water to keep their 55-foot keelboat afloat. Even with the addition of dams to store spring runoff, the Missouri we paddled should have been shallow and full of sandbars. Instead, the river ran at minor flood stage six months after spring runoff began.

Total runoff for the year nearly matched the devastating floods of 2011, yet precipitation was more evenly distributed through the season. The U.S. Army Corps of Engineers uses its system of dams to hold back the surges, metering out water as necessary to make room for future storms. With so much water in the reservoirs, big releases and minor flooding were necessary to prevent major flooding later.

Jubilee is growing up on the canoe, now having lived half her life on the adventure.

Paddling past riverfront homes in Verdel, Nebraska, most houses appeared dry, while some were temporarily abandoned and surrounded by shallow water. Moving closer for a better look, John paddled through yards and over lawns.

We found dry land to camp in a small coulee behind a cattail swamp across the river. The guys caught several small-mouth bass for a delicious fried fish dinner and breakfast. Dusk brought the tremolo of a nearby pair of screech owls, followed shortly afterwards by the hoo-hoo of two great-horned owls. Coyotes followed the chorus, as if our little coulee was the local amphitheater for nightlife. Crickets maintained ambient forest sounds to lull us to sleep.

Approaching the Niobrara River, the Missouri thickened into a maze of sandbars and swamps. William Clark recorded the river's name in French as "Que Courre," meaning the river that runs. The name Niobrara now in use is a corruption of the Omaha-Ponca name Ní Ubthátha khe, meaning "The Wide-Spreading River." As Clark noted, the river throws sand into the Missouri, forming a morass of sandbars.

We enjoyed some beautiful fish for dinner.

199

Lewis and Clark Lake is quickly being filled in with sandbars and vegetation.

This year's flood cycle started with a "bomb cyclone" in March that dropped heavy rain and snow on frozen ground across the Great Plains. Unable to penetrate frozen soil, water flowed overland, covering half the state of Nebraska in standing water. Flood waters washed out Spencer Dam on the Niobrara River. An eleven-foot wall of water swept away farms and livestock, washed out bridges, and flooded the town of Niobrara.

A few miles below the Niobrara River, the 39-mile upper portion of the Missouri National Recreational River is separated from the 59-mile lower portion by Lewis and Clark Lake and Gavins Point Dam. This is the last dam on the Missouri, with a reservoir only fifteen miles long.

Hatched turtle eggs.

Snowy egrets perch on a log.

Like all reservoirs, sediment settles out as the river turns to lake. With the Niobrara contributing so much sand to the Missouri, Lewis and Clark Lake is already 30 percent full, forming a jungle-like maze of sandbars overgrown with head-high phragmites, or common reed grass. Thanks to high water and the incoming river current, we were able to negotiate the maze through larger channels, only once dragging the heavy dugout canoe over a submerged sandbar. Miles later, we reached an open lake lined by cliff walls of brightly colored chalkstone. The orange and white hues reminded me of a vanilla-orange dreamsicle, such is the fantasy world of a hungry paddler.

River current flows miles into the lake as the scenery transitions from sandbars to open water and chalkstone bluffs.

Paddling into the sunrise.

Morning light brings out the colors in the chalkstone bluffs.

Although beautiful, we find ourselves challenged by the lake paddling.

A turkey vulture warms itself in the sun.

The scenic cliffs were cleaved off by waves from the artificial lake lapping at the hillsides.

We took a break for lunch and fishing.

We camped at Sand Creek Recreation Area, where I experimented with duckweed (*Lemna*) for dinner, which I harvested at the previous night's campsite. The tiny swamp plants were blended with wild rice and wrapped in tortillas to hide a slightly swampy flavor and texture.

The next day we paddled the remaining thirteen miles to Gavins point. For our crew, paddling the short lake was sufficient reminder that we greatly prefer floating with the river current. There are fifteen dams on the Missouri, including five in a row that are necessarily portaged as one at Great Falls, Montana. Of the remaining ten reservoirs, we paddled six and motored four. Gavins Point Dam was the final obstacle.

Local river angel Jaret Bies met us with the canoe trailer and helped us portage to Chief White Crane Recreation Area below the dam. He

Jaret Bies (second from right) helped us portage the dam.

generously loaned us his car the following day to navigate the nearby town of Yankton, South Dakota. After completing essential errands, Scott and I toured the *Journeying Forward* exhibit at the Dakota Territorial Museum. It was a traveling exhibit created by American Rivers for the bicentennial celebration of the 1803 - 1806 Lewis and Clark Expedition, later gifted to the Yankton County Historical Society.

In the morning we hiked up to the Lewis and Clark Visitor Center overlooking the dam, trying not to miss anything important. And finally, we launched down the river. With the dams behind us, we looked forward to flowing river all the way to St. Louis!

Scott and I toured the Journeying Forward: Connecting Cultures exhibit at the Mead Cultural Education Center in Yankton.

Sand burrs (Cenchrus longispinus) are sharp and evil!

A traditional bullboat paddle on display at the U.S. Army Corps of Engineers Gavins Point Project Lewis & Clark Visitor Center.

Gavins Point Dam released 80,000 CFS from Lewis and Clark Lake.

Jubilee has her favorite spot in the bow with her papa.

205

Sunrise on the Missouri National Recreational River.

Dead trees are preferred perches for raptors.

Photo by Scott Robinson

Chris and I swapped seating each day in the canoe.

It's a wide, wide river.

"We Came to [to] make a warm bath for Sergt. Floyd hopeing it would brace him a little, before we could get him in to this bath he expired, with a great deel of composure, haveing Said to me before his death that he was going away and wished me to write a letter— we Buried him to the top of a high round hill over looking the river & Countrey for a great distance   Situated just below a Small river without a name to which we name & call Floyds river, the Bluffs Sergts. Floyds Bluff—we buried him with all the honors of War, and fixed a Ceeder post at his head with his name title & Day of the month and year."

—William Clark, August 20, 1804

Channeling Floyd

Judging from the raging torrent of 80,000 cubic feet per second pouring out of Gavins Point Dam, it seemed like we might be in for a wild ride down the Missouri. Yet the current settled down to a mild 4 to 5 mph by the time it reached the boat ramp, a mere mile downstream from the dam. Here began the 59-mile lower portion of the Missouri National Recreational River, another fragment of the river that remains largely unchanged since the time of Lewis and Clark, aside from houses along the river bank.

Muddy grass from recent flooding doesn't compare to the vastly deeper flooding of 2011.

Paddling flood waters can be highly dangerous in Montana where narrow, winding streams turn into roiling rivers, but the Missouri is so big it is like a slow-moving lake. Minor flooding makes it a bigger slow-moving lake. The storm that dropped two inches of rain on us at Lake Sharpe hit southeastern South Dakota with a whopping nine inches of rain, causing major flooding on the James River, which pours into the Missouri downstream from Yankton. We tracked flood reports online, and fortunately, the big trees and other flood debris flushed out ahead of us. Water levels were already receding by the time we reached the confluence with the James.

Paddling a slow-moving lake has its own challenges. Think of a canoe and paddle as analogous to a car and steering wheel, providing the illusion of control as you travel down the highway. When paddling, however, the road itself is moving. That's easy enough if the river is narrow and the current moves predictably downstream. But the Missouri is so wide that the current snakes back and forth unpredictably within the river, sometimes doubling back upstream right in the middle.

Acorns carpet the trails at Ponca State Park.

Looking ahead at a big cottonwood snag in the river, it seemed like we would drift past on the right with ample room to spare Moments later we would be aiming past it on the left. We could paddle the entire time, thinking we were headed one direction while the river took us another. At the last moment, we could be flowing rapidly sideways towards the only tree in the river. Add a breeze, and there were four variables of motion: river, current, paddling, and wind. Dodging a snag was easy enough with a few quick power strokes, but control over our overall trajectory was illusory.

We completed the recreational river in two days, arriving at Ponca State Park in Nebraska. Strands of the eastern deciduous forest follow the river north through the prairie, creating an oasis of bur oak trees, black walnut, hackberry, mulberry, and linden or basswood, with a rich understory of diverse eastern vegetation. One old oak tree has been growing since at least 1644. A scenic overlook allows a view of Nebraska, South Dakota, and Iowa. I had hoped to stay two nights at the state park, but turbulent weather in the forecast prodded us to paddle while we could.

Evening sun filters through the trees along a hiking trail.

Below Ponca State Park the Missouri River has been narrowed, deepened, and straightened as a channel all the way to St. Louis. The river has been shortened by nearly 200 miles since the time of Lewis and Clark. Despite our expectations of swift current, the river still ran at 3 to 5 mph.

The channel was admittedly much easier to paddle than the natural river. We stayed away from wing dams, wooden pylons, and submerged trees along the bank, preferring to stick to the middle and drift or paddle with the current. However, strange boils rose up out of nowhere, like underwater geysers that sent circular currents out to deflect the canoe one direction or another. The sudden turbulence and sound of crashing water was perpetually unnerving, yet seemingly harmless. Intermittent mile markers counted down the remaining distance to Saint Louis.

One day's paddle brought us to the Missouri's confluence with the Big Sioux River, marking the border between South Dakota and Iowa. Sioux City in Iowa is joined by North Sioux City in South Dakota and South Sioux City in Nebraska to make a modest conglomerate city bridging three states.

We camped at the Scenic Park Campground on the Nebraska side. My friend Chuck Hopp gave us a great tour of the area. In the evening we played a game of *Wildlife Web* at a fast food establishment in town.

Sioux City was founded by Theophile Bruguier, a trader with the American Fur Company who married two daughters of Chief War Eagle of the Yankton Sioux and built a cabin there in 1849. Sioux City is also the burial

New England asters (Symphyotrichum novae-angliae) are crazy colorful.

The "Towers of Time" sculpture by Jay Tschetter depicts the region's natural and native history.

209

The Big Sioux River, shown in the foreground, merges with the Missouri, bringing yet more water to the already flooded river.

place of Sergeant Charles Floyd, who gained fame largely by keeling over of "bilious colic," which medical experts theorize was likely appendicitis. Floyd's accomplishment is aggrandized by his being the only member of the Corps of Discovery to die on the expedition. While there were many near-death accidents and some tense stand-offs with tribes along the route, nobody died except Floyd, and his death was pre-ordained by a medical condition for which there was no cure. It is a good reminder that every day is precious, and we never really know when our time is up.

Lewis and Clark buried Floyd on a hill and named it Floyd's Bluff, along with the nearby Floyd's River, then they proceeded on with their journey. I like the simplicity of that, and if I were to keel over, I would prefer that the crew bury me on a bluff along the river. Just wrap me in a wool blanket and include my hand-carved paddle and maybe some books from my floating library to read in the afterlife. It's not like I need those items, but it would be a respectful send off before finishing the journey to paddle Belladonna Beaver to St. Louis.

Theophile Bruguier's cabin, built in 1849.

Sadly, we've made the modern world so complicated and expensive it would be near impossible to continue the journey if I, or anyone, died. Laws forbid simple burials along the river. Instead, there would be an investigation and coroner's report followed by cremation or embalming to ship the remains back home. The average funeral now costs $7,000 to $10,000 as we saturate our loved ones with toxic chemicals and bury them in steel caskets where they slowly bleed contaminants into the groundwater.

Even poor Floyd hardly got any rest. His grave had been disturbed, possibly by wolves, before the Corps of Discovery revisited the site on their 1806 return trip, so they refilled the hole. By 1857 the shifting river began to erode his grave, so concerned citizens dug him up and reburied him 200 yards away. The publishing of Sergeant Floyd's journal in 1894 inspired folks to dig up his remaining remains and bury them in urns under a marble slab. Then he was moved again while the Floyd Memorial Association upgraded his grave to a 100-foot-tall sandstone obelisk, completed in 1901.

Sergeant Floyd is memorialized by a 100-foot tall sandstone obelisk.

Fur trapping display in the Sergeant Floyd River Museum & Welcome Center.

While his remains were in storage during construction, volunteers weighed, measured, and photographed his bones and made a plaster cast of his skull. With the aid of modern forensics, visitors can now see a close approximation of Floyd in the Sergeant Floyd Museum and Welcome Center aboard the dry-docked motor vessel, the *M.V. Sergeant Floyd*.

The adjacent Lewis and Clark Interpretive Center went one step further, channeling Floyd from beyond the grave as a silicone and silicon animatronic member of the Corps of Discovery, sharing reflections about his life and untimely death.

Sergeant Floyd isn't alone. Thomas Jefferson is there to welcome visitors, while Lewis and Clark stand over Floyd's coffin in the back room, talking up his good character. When Floyd whispered his dying words that he was "going away," he probably never imagined that he would keep coming back.

Charles Floyd greets visitors as an animatronic being.

Animatronic Clark and Lewis discuss the passing of Sergeant Charles Floyd at the Sioux City Lewis and Clark Interpretive Center.

Tightly packed grains of loess soil remain fairly stable even when vertically cleaved, however a footpath can quickly erode into a gully.

Loessens in Soil and Geography

Ice Age glaciers ground underlying bedrock into a fine powder known as "glacial flour." Melting ice released sediment-rich floods down the Missouri River, which dried to form mud flats of fine silt. Winds blew the silt across the Midwest, forming dunes or hills near the river and flats far beyond, known today as loess soil. Ten thousand years of accumulated organic humus helped build fertile prairie topsoil, which can be easily eroded to expose the underlying loess. The fine grains of loess soil weather rapidly, releasing mineral nutrients that allow continued harvests even in highly erosive conditions.

Loess soils form the main surface strata following the Missouri and Mississippi rivers almost to the Gulf of Mexico. As seen from the river, however, loess soils are prominent along the Nebraska border from Ponca State Park downstream to White Cloud, Kansas. Loess soils form the hills and bluffs that keep towns and cities above the meandering river channel. Without the loess hills, this portion of the river basin would be mostly flat and featureless.

Chuck Hopp helped build this prairie soil exhibit at the Dorothy Pecaut Nature Center.

Passing under the I-129 bridge perpendicular to the river.

The expedition used woven willow nets to catch fish.

"I went with ten men to a Creek Damed by the Beavers about half way to the Village, with Some Small willow & Bark we mad a Drag and haulted up the Creek, and Cought 318 fish of different kind i'e' Peke, Bass, Salmon, perch, red horse, Small Cat, and a kind of perch Called Silverfish, on the Ohio."

—William Clark, August 15, 1804

Fish Stories

We blew out of Sioux City with the wind, or rather, against it, facing a stiff headwind as our only opportunity to move downstream before yet another storm rolled through. The headwind made it near impossible to steer the canoes. Front-heavy Belladonna Beaver turned perpendicular to the river and wouldn't turn back. Chris and I drifted along sideways staring at the riverbank while Jubilee whined about the wind and waves. Scott's canoe also drifted sideways, while John's shorter, wider canoe drifted backwards, none of us able to paddle except toward or away from either shore.

Ten miles south of Sioux City we passed by Fish Camp, where the Corps of Discovery camped August 13-19, 1804 to invite the Otoe an Omaha Indians to council. In their spare time, the men wove willows together to make a stiff net that they dragged up the stream, catching 318 fish one day, and nearly 800 fish the next day. Using a similar method along the Beaverhead River in Montana a year later, they caught 512 fish. It seems unlikely those methods would yield comparable results today due to degradation of fish habitat.

Some native species are endangered, while many new fish have been introduced, including multiple species of carp. Although carp are disdained by Americans, they are considered a delicacy in other parts of the world and often served as a Christmas dish in Eastern European countries. I hunted carp with a fishing bow and arrow the first week of the trip, anticipating carp all the way downriver, but didn't find other suitable places to hunt.

Scott and John have been the serious fishermen of the trip, catching mostly small mouth bass, northern pike, goldeye, walleye, and perch. They had great success on Fort Peck Lake in Montana followed by long lapses as we've moved downstream. The high water year seems to be a factor, as other fishermen were also striking out.

I anticipated eating fish as daily fare on this adventure, and I was worried about cumulative mercury and PCB levels due to fish consumption advisories. Mercury contamination comes from coal-fired power plants, mining and industrial wastes, batteries, and household waste. PCBs (polychlorinated bipenyls) were used in lubricants, coolants, ink, and paint until banned in 1977, but remain persistent in the environment.

Lewis and Clark actually brought mercury as medicine. Prior to germ theory, medical philosophy emphasized removing bad humors or morbid elements from the body. Mercury was one of the ingredients in Rush's pills, a powerful cathartic otherwise known as "thunderclappers." Mercury was also injected in the penis or anus to treat venereal disease and other ailments. The Corps of Discovery consumed enough mercury that archaeologists can verify Lewis and Clark campsites by testing for mercury in the soil from their latrines.

George Neal Energy Center coal-fired power plant.

I expected to get a Lewis and Clark sized dose of mercury by eating fish for five months, but fortunately we had no such luck. Instead of fish, we've eaten store-bought beef, pork, and chicken, ensuring a well-rounded diet of growth hormones and antibiotics to complement the mercury and PCBs. Add nitrates from a lifetime worth of summer sausage, and we are models of healthy living in the twenty-first century.

With the river flowing at 5 mph, we made good time downriver. An afternoon lull in the wind allowed us to orient the canoes and paddle with the current, attaining 7 mph. A forty-mile day brought us to Decatur, Nebraska to camp at the Beck and Busse Memorial Recreation Area.

Receding flood waters hatched a legion of mosquitoes to torment us. The campground flooded three times this year, according to the park manager, with recent flooding evident where the grass was still muddy brown. He advised us to move our tents onto the concrete slab inside the group shelter on the highest part of the property to wait out the latest deluge.

Scott paddles under the all-metal bridge at Decatur.

215

Dan Hurd is paddling 48 states for suicide awareness (www.ridewithdanusa.com).

Bullboat and paddle.

Try dragging the keelboat up against the current.

Inside the captains' quarters on the keelboat.

There we met Dan Hurd, who is taking three years to bicycle the lower forty-eight states to promote suicide awareness. Nebraska was state number thirty-three after nineteen months and 14,000 miles traveling north and south with the seasons.

Dan joined Scott and I the following day to hitch a ride across the bridge to Lewis and Clark State Park in Iowa. The park houses a full-size keelboat replica as well as two wooden boats or pirogues, one white and one red, presumably like those of the expedition.

Coming from Montana, where the Corps of Discovery consisted of eight dugout canoes, I hadn't grasped the scale of the expedition until I stood on the keelboat. It was a real ship! Another large keelboat is used on the lake within the park, but was already dry-docked for winter.

Lewis and Clark State Park in Iowa houses a full-size replica keelboat like that used by the Corps of Discovery.

My last jar of canned fruit.

Minor flooding is pervasive along the river.

I had packed several jars of canned fruit in the bowels of my canoe, which I had replenished from a resupply box back at Fort Peck in July. I saved the pie cherries for last, serving them on pancakes. That was a delicious treat.

The rain subsided after two nights in Decatur, raising the flooded river by nearly a foot. We paddled downstream to the town of Blair while Dan bicycled ahead of us. By the time we arrived, he had obtained permission for us to camp at the Optimist Park, plus he called the local newspaper and a television station from Omaha to report on his story and ours.

Local river angel Steve Stodola saw our canoes and drove by to offer whatever assistance we needed. He taxied us to Kelly's Fish Market for dinner. I ordered the carp, having never seen it on a restaurant menu before. Proprietor Mike Kelly caught it himself on the Niobrara River. His batter-fried carp was truly gourmet!

Thinking back to Lewis and Clark, they brought 2,500 fishhooks for gifts and trade with Native Americans, sometimes even bartering hooks for fish to eat. They bought fish for dinner, and so did we.

A deluge of fresh rain rose the river level and washed Belladonna Beaver shiny clean.

We have begun encountering tow boats and barges parked along the flooded river. We otherwise have the river to ourselves.

Mile markers count down the remaining distance to the confluence.

A cottonwood tree, half alive, half dead.

I ordered batter-fried carp at Kelly's Fish Market.

Sunrise at Blair, Nebraska.

Cranes load a barge near Omaha.

Approaching the big city of Omaha.

Passing beyond the Interstate 680 bridge.

Circumstances required camping at Freedom Park.

"The Situation of our last Camp Councill Bluff or Handssom Prarie appears to be a verry proper place for a Tradeing establishment & fortification   The Soil of the Bluff well adapted for Brick, Great deel of timbers above in the two Points. many other advantages of a Small nature.   and I am told Senteral to Several nations   Viz. one Days march from the Ottoe Town, one Day & a half from the great Pania village, 2 days from the Mahar Towns, two ¼ Days from the Loups Village, & Convenient to the Countrey thro: which Bands of the Soux hunt."

—*William Clark, August 3, 1804*

Water World

William Clark's vision for a fort at Council Bluff was realized fifteen years later when Col. Henry Atkinson led an expedition of 1,120 men to build a string of forts along the Missouri River. Their trial steamboats floundered against the river's currents, sandbars, and snags, making Council Bluff the terminus of the expedition. The soldiers constructed a substantial, but short-lived fort in the woodlands below the bluff. Severe winter conditions contributed to scurvy, claiming the lives of 160 men, followed by record high spring runoff that flooded the fort and necessitated reconstruction on top of the bluff, per Clark's original recommendations.

Fort Atkinson served as the gateway to the fur trade, becoming the first U.S. military post west of the Missouri River, and the largest fort in the country. Westward colonization brought an end to the fort by 1827. It was reconstructed in the 1980s and 90s as Fort Atkinson State Historical Park.

The Missouri River long ago shifted three miles east of the fort, while ongoing flood conditions made landing impossible, so we paddled downriver to Omaha and caught a ride back.

Finding a dry and legal place to camp near Omaha proved problematic. Our friend Dan bicycled ahead to research possible sites downtown, but without success. Chris, Scott, and I stopped to assess our options by Freedom Park, a Naval museum featuring a ship, submarine, jet and other military hardware. Unable to locate any

I hid my tent between two green army trucks for camouflage.

A re-enactor fires the cannon at Fort Atkinson State Historical Park.

Re-enactors shared strawberry pie cooked in a Dutch oven.

Solitary confinement boxes reveal frontier discipline.

place to camp legally, we ultimately pitched tents within the park, which was otherwise closed due to flooding. Scott called it, "the coolest campsite ever." I hid my green tent between two green army trucks grown over with grass, vines, and brush, as if hiding out in a post-apocalyptic era.

John, meanwhile, paddled onward, bound for the finish line in St. Louis. I was sorry to lose him from the expedition, but he was urgently needed back home. The rest of us hunkered down for another major thunderstorm that dropped a couple inches of rain, but thankfully tapered off by morning. We hiked uptown and caught a ride to Fort Atkinson with Mary Langhorst of the Mouth of the Platte Chapter of the Lewis and Clark Trail Heritage Foundation. Mary is part of a small army of volunteers who offer living history demonstrations at Fort Atkinson one weekend per month.

Paul Siebert plays a gourd banjo.

Although Fort Atkinson was a military post, it's location far from civilization necessitated self-sufficiency, and most soldiers were employed tending crops and livestock. Re-enactors fired the canon, skinned and processed a bison, demonstrated blacksmithing, tinwork, and Dutch oven cooking, among dozens of activities. Scott and Dan jumped in on

223

the pie-eating contest. Local survival instructors Doug Carlson and Rod Vanhorn joined us in the afternoon and later gave us a ride back to Omaha.

Lewis and Clark National Historic Trail office.

Hiking down the railroad tracks past homeless camps towards our riverside hideout, I too felt homeless. Hiding out like fugitives among the bushes and defunct military equipment gnawed on my nerves. Did anyone ransack or steal our tents or canoes? Would we get in trouble for camping in the closed park? Wading through the flooded access road and mud to get to our mosquito-infested camp amid the flood debris, I wondered if conditions might continue this way to St. Louis.

In the morning we paddled down to Riverfront Marina, which was also closed due to flooding, but parked our canoes and climbed over the fence to tour the town. We enjoyed a short visit next door at National Park Service headquarters for the Lewis and Clark National Historic Trail.

Dan arranged a Lyft® to the Western Historic Trails Center on the Iowa side in Council Bluffs, the city having been named after Clark's bluffs at Fort Atkinson. Keith Bystrom of the Mouth of the Platte Chapter LCTHF met us there and gave us a royal tour of the area, plus a savory lunch at a Mexican restaurant. Lewis and Clark Park provided a great view over the Missouri River, including Interstate 25, which was recently closed due to flooding.

Floodwaters recently closed Interstate 29, as seen here from Lewis and Clark Monument Park and Scenic Overlook.

Keith Bystrom gave us a great tour of the area.

Back on the river, we paddled to Haworth Park Campground by Bellevue, which was entirely flooded except for half the parking lot by the submerged boat ramp. We pitched our tents on the asphalt. The nearby Children's Lewis & Clark Interpretive Art Wall tells the Corps of Discovery story in hand-painted tiles created by school kids grades 3 through 6 from communities along the trail. It is a fantastic mural featuring hundreds of artful tiles.

The morning sun brought local police to investigate our tents in the closed campground, but they accepted our need for a safe campsite and wished us well. Flooding is widespread, but not deep enough to wash houses off their foundations into the river. A few small outbuildings and some campers moved short distances, lodging in adjacent trees, but mostly the river is lined with houses and campers on tiny islands surrounded by water or sitting in shallow water.

I can imagine folks cleaning up after spring flooding and putting their lives back together, but it's been six months of repeated flooding with no end of sight. Early snowfall on saturated soils across the Rocky Mountains and Great Plains hints

Seeds drift from a milkweed seed pod.

Children created hundreds of ceramic tiles for a mural of the Lewis and Clark story.

We are beginning to see fall colors, here likely caused by prolonged flooding.

Scores of campers were caught in the mud.

Gauges on each bridge mark clearance, not depth, here indicating 50 feet of clearance for ships.

Floodwaters sweep toxic trash into the river.

at more flooding to come. Rather than a post-apocalyptic world, it seemed like a pre-apocalyptic glimpse of the new normal in a climate-changed world.

Riverview Marina State Park at Nebraska City was completely underwater. We tied off at the grain elevators in town and caught a ride with Keith back to his house for a fabulous steak dinner then camped in his yard. We toured the Lewis and Clark Visitor Center in the morning, which featured a great exhibit about fishing on the Expedition.

Lewis brought Seaman, his Newfoundland dog.

I signed books at the visitor center.

Lewis brought medicines like these.

A day of paddling brought us to Brownville, where the bridge had been closed since March due to flood damage to the access road, severely impacting business in town. We didn't see boats on the river for days, not because it was particularly dangerous, but because there wasn't any means to get boats on or off the river when every boat ramp and marina was closed due to flooding. It was safe enough to paddle down the channel, giving wide berth to breaks in the levees where swift currents exited or re-entered the main channel.

Nevertheless, I couldn't help but feel a constant state of mild anxiety paddling through this flooded world, with the river six feet above flood stage. The boat ramp at Indian Cave State Park consisted of another parking lot surrounded by water. The park manager said we were

The Brownville bridge has been closed for months due to flood damage.

Sunrise from Brownville, Nebraska.

crazy, sloshing down the road through foot-deep water to ask about camping. But she instructed us to paddle around to a bay where we found the perfect campsite to weather another storm.

Hiking up to a scenic vantage point, I saw for first time that the river extended two or three miles beyond the river channel. I wondered if we should have followed John's lead and paddled like crazy for the end.

Paw paw (Asimina triloba)

Scott walks the flooded road to the boat ramp after meeting with the park ranger.

Flooding extends far beyond the narrow river channel we see from our canoes. Sumac leaves turn color in the park.

But at Indian Cave there were great trails to explore and a whole new ecological zone dominated by sycamore trees, shagbark hickory, at least two species of oak, and paw-paw trees everywhere. As a botanist-forager-survivalist, finding ripe paw-paws was a highlight of the journey. The raw fruits have a taste and texture similar to banana custard. I canned four quarts of fruit, wishing I had sufficient time and resources to can fifty quarts to bring home to Montana. For me, it was experiences like this that made the whole trip worthwhile.

Shagbark hickory (Carya ovata)

My friend Dean Zimmerman and his cousin Norm paddled Bella around the bay.

I canned four quarts of paw paws to take home, wishing I could do many more.

Park employees deploy thousands of decorations for Halloween festivities.

I enjoyed hiking the trails at Indian Cave State Park.

A dead cottonwood towers over all else.

Kansas - Missouri

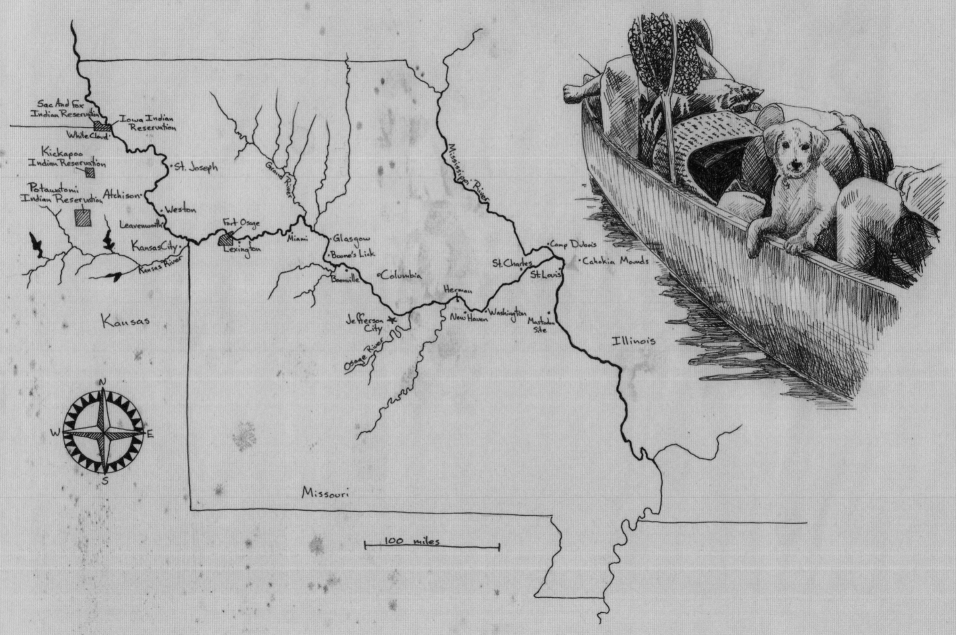

Sac And Fox Indian Reservation

Iowa Indian Reservation

White Cloud

Kickapoo Indian Reservation

Potawatomi Indian Reservation

Atchison

St. Joseph

Weston

Leavenworth

Fort Osage

Kansas City

Lexington

Miami

Glasgow

Boone's Lick

Boonville

Columbia

Kansas River

Grand River

Kansas

Camp Dubois

Cahokia Mounds

St. Charles

St. Louis

Herman

Jefferson City

New Haven

Washington

Mastodon Site

Osage River

Illinois

Mississippi River

Missouri

100 miles

N
W E
S

"A verry warm day (worthy of remark that the water of this river or Some other Cause, I think that the most Probable throws out a greater preposn. of Swet than I could Suppose Could pass thro: the humane body   Those men that do not work at all will wet a Shirt in a Few minits & those who work, the Swet will run off in Streams)."

—William Clark, July 6, 1804

Cold Front

"You're lucky you weren't here a few days ago when it was 95°F and humid," Deb said, echoing the conditions Lewis and Clark experienced while ascending this stretch of the river in mid-summer.

Our last storm at Indian Cave State Park brought only light rain, but temperatures dropped precipitously in its wake. We were at the southern edge of a cold front that brought heavy snow and frigid temperatures up north, including two feet of snow in my hometown of Pony, Montana. We were migrating south, trying to stay ahead of the changing seasons, but near-freezing temperatures and cold wind announced the end of summer vacation.

We paddled away from Indian Cave with a strong tailwind, largely ameliorated by heavy tree cover along the banks. Less than ten miles later we hit a treeless stretch with a side wind that blew us against the only patch of dry ground on the flooded river. Taking shelter for the rest of the day, I started and nearly finished reading *Bury My Heart at Wounded Knee*. The book details the Indian Wars from the perspective of the conquered, rather than the conquerors. It should be required reading for all students of American History.

Paddling conditions were vastly better by dawn. A hot water bottle in a reflective grocery sack kept my feet warm through the chilly morning, and the afternoon was comfortable enough. Local river angel Deborah Bryan tracked our progress online, greeting us at the boat ramp moments after we arrived in White Cloud, Kansas. Deb invited us to stay in the old general

Deb Bryan gave us a great tour of White Cloud and the surrounding area.

233

Flooding extends miles beyond the Missouri River channel.

Morning reflection of the grain elevator on the river.

This Iowa bear claw necklace, on display the casino, was handed down through the White Cloud family.

store she is restoring on Main Street. She is working on several buildings and leading the effort to revitalize the community. We enjoyed hot stew from the crockpot, and Deb gave us an extensive tour of the area.

Her great-great-great grandfather was Chief Ma-Has-Ka, or White Cloud of the Iowa Tribe. The state of Iowa, named for the tribe, was once entirely Iowa tribal territory. The Iowas lost territory to white settlement as well as to increased competition from other tribes who were equally squeezed by westward expansion. In 1836 White Cloud signed a treaty with William Clark in which the Iowa, Sac, and Fox tribes moved west of the Missouri River, granting lands on the east side to white settlement.

White Cloud reportedly climbed a hill to pray for guidance and found plantain (*Plantago major*) growing in abundance. Indians knew the plant as "white man's footsteps," because it grew wherever the white man went. Seeing it well-established there, White Cloud signed the treaty and moved his people across the river. Deb hopes to meet Churchill Clark, who helped me carve the dugout canoe. As the fourth-great grandson of William Clark, the two descendants could shake hands in a renewal of peaceful relations for another generation.

River conditions greatly improved below White Cloud, with fewer breaches in the levy system. I relaxed for the first time in days, comforted by the sight of nearly continuous dry ground on both sides of the river channel. Light motorboat traffic hinted at functional boat ramps for access. A pleasant day of paddling brought us to St. Joseph, where river angels Emma Gossett and Derrick Boos waved us into town, generously treated us to dinner, and showed us around the town.

Deb had arranged permission to pitch our tents at the port, which was a great campsite, providing easy access to downtown St. Joseph. However, we returned to find three inches of water in the dugout canoe, thanks to a passing sand barge. Sand is dredged from the river bottom upstream for a concrete plant located a short distance downstream. I bailed out the canoe, hoping it wouldn't happen again. We stayed long enough in the morning to tour the home where Jesse James was shot and killed in 1882, meeting up briefly with Bicycle

The sand barge passed back and forth past our canoes.

Paddles are handy for passing sandwiches around.

Broadleaf plantain (Plantago major) was known as "white man's footsteps."

The Pony Express operated for only eighteen months, but lives forever in the legacy of the West. Courtesy of Pony Express National Museum.

The wake of the barge turned our canoes into bucking broncos. Chris went for a cold dip to retrieve his dry bag.

Dan, who had been riding parallel to our route. We also toured the Pony Express Museum, learning about the legendary mail service that employed 120 riders, 184 way stations, 400 horses, and hundreds of additional employees to provide fast and reliable communication between St. Joseph, Missouri and Sacramento, California. The Pony Express opened in April of 1860 and closed eighteen months later, eclipsed by nearly instant telegraph service.

All packed up and ready to leave town, we stood on the riverbank while the sand barge passed by, it's massive wake riling the canoes into bucking broncos on the water. Chris's dry bag bounced off into the river, and he sprang into action, diving flat onto the canoe, then over into the roiling waters to catch the bag. I bailed six inches of water out the canoe while he put on dry clothes. An otherwise pleasant day brought us to Atchison, Kansas, where we obtained permission through the police department to pitch our tents on the narrow strip of grass between the road and the boat ramp.

Bicycle Dan showed up in the morning with Wendy Maupin of Weston, Missouri, who recognized Dan in town from our online posts. Wendy previously visited Montana while our mutual friend Churchill was staying at my house, and now we were in her neighborhood. We toured the Amelia Earhart Birthplace Museum on the bluff above town. Looking out over the river, I wondered if that aerial view inspired Earhart's interest in flying.

Wendy and Dan brought a kayak and joined us for an almost-warm day on the water, flying downstream at 6 mph. Local river angel Larry Caster invited us to camp at his riverfront cabin near Salt Creek. The structure was built on pylons above the ground, but spring flood waters still ran several feet deep through the house. Larry and wife Annette

Purple morning glory (Ipomoea purpurea)

The Amelia Earhart Bridge lights up the Missouri River at night.

We toured the Amelia Earhart Birthplace Museum in Atchison, Kansas.

Amelia Earhart model greets visitors at the museum.

Dan Hurd and Wendy Maupin joined us on the river for a day of paddling. Here's another power plant.

Bush Honeysuckle (Lonicera maackii)

Weston, Missouri is a popular western-themed tourist town.

Wendy Maupin gave a great tour of the town.

laboriously cleaned up the mud, but haven't fully refurnished the building. The access road was washed out by a new channel cut through a breach in the levy system, rendering the cabin inaccessible except by boat. We enjoyed a relaxing afternoon around the fire before Larry, Wendy, and Dan all headed downriver, and we sought shelter inside, grateful for solid walls against the cold breeze.

Paddling to Bee Creek at dawn, Wendy picked us up for a tour of historic Weston. Weston was a major river port until the flood of 1881 shifted the main river channel two miles to the west, leaving the town high and dry.

Back on the water in the afternoon, we paddled another fifteen miles, tied the canoes at the river bank and caught a ride back to Wendy's house to sleep. The chill of autumn nights was more than offset by the warm hospitality of folks all along the Missouri River. After four and half months living as vagabonds, we were ready for some civilized comforts.

Fall colors are starting to pop on some of the trees.

Buttonbush
(Cephalanthus occidentalis)

Pokeweed
(Phytolacca americana)

Poison ivy vines (Toxicodendron radicans) climb trees.

"Set out from the Kansas river ½ past 4 oClock, proceeded on passed a Small run on the L. S. at ½ Mile a Island on the S. S. at 1½ me. Hills above the upr. pt of Isd. L. S. a large Sand bar in the middle. Passed a verry bad place of water, the Sturn of the Boat Struck a moveing Sand & turned within 6 Inches of a large Sawyer, if the Boat had Struck the Sawyer, her Bow must have been Knocked off & in Course She must hav Sunk in the Deep water below."

—William Clark, June 29, 1804

Sawyers

We stopped at Lewis and Clark Park at Kaw Point at the Missouri's confluence with the Kansas River.

The untamed Missouri formed a minefield of sawyers or snags, dead trees anchored to the bottom. Colliding with a sawyer could have sunk the keelboat and ended the Lewis and Clark Expedition at any point on the Missouri. The rise of steamboat technology soon led to a commercial boom up the Missouri River, but it remained a treacherous journey. Between boiler explosions and sawyers, steamboats rarely survived for five years. An estimated 400 steamboats sunk on the Missouri before railroads provided a safe and economical alternative in the late 1800s.

Passing under the I-29 Christopher S. Bond Bridge.

Navigating today's channelized river is vastly easier, although it does have its own challenges. We hoped to camp in the middle of Kansas City for easy access to town. Helpful folks on the Missouri River Paddlers Group on Facebook offered eighty comments with pros and cons regarding safety and legal issues for potential camping options near the city. With the forecast calling for a good day followed by a windy day, we opted to paddle through the city and catch a ride back. Wendy Maupin joined us for half a day, exiting the river to work in town.

Kansas City is technically two separate cities, one in Kansas, the other in Missouri, separated by the Kansas River that marks the boundary between the two states. We stopped briefly at the confluence at Kaw Point Park where Lewis and Clark camped June 26 - 28, 1804 for respite and to repair their boats.

241

We toured the Arabia Steamboat Museum.

The Arabia was filled with thousands of trade items for frontier merchants.

River angel Bill Fessler graciously invited us to camp at his recreation cabin downstream near Orrick, in spite of extensive flood damage there. During the height of the flood, Bill kayaked through his own cabin. Now the water was down, and the grass was green, yet mucking out the house remained a daunting project. Nevertheless, Bill fired up the barbecue grill and greeted us with hamburgers. We enjoyed a pleasant evening around the campfire with Bill and friend John.

The Arabia Steamboat Museum was a must-see in Kansas City as we toured the town with Bill. The Arabia was headed upstream in September of 1856 with 130 passengers and 220 tons of cargo when it hit a sawyer and sank. Fortunately, the upper decks remained above water, allowing rescue of all passengers. Whiskey kegs

Wool and leather clothing survived in like-new condition.

Trade beads were rescued from the ship.

and other cargo on the lower deck were swept away with the river, but everything in the cargo hold was preserved in a watery time capsule. The boat continued sinking deeper into the muddy riverbed for years until the river shifted course, leaving the Arabia forty-five feet below ground in what later became a cornfield.

The approximate location was retained over time, but accessing the ship below ground and below the water table stymied early recovery efforts. In 1988, amateur treasure hunters Bob Hawley and sons obtained landowner permission to excavate the Arabia, partnering with friends Jerry Mackey and David Luttrell on the enterprise. The ship itself was largely beyond salvage, the upper decks having been ravaged by the river, but they recovered the engine, boilers and paddlewheel core. The real treasure was the merchandise in the cargo hold, originally destined for resale in frontier towns.

The team salvaged the world's largest collection of pre-civil war artifacts, totaling hundreds of thousands of items, including saws, axe heads, hinges, dishes, silverware, beads, and clothing. Vegetable fibers, such as cotton, degraded over time, but animal proteins, such as leather and wool, survived in like-new condition. Although the team intended to sell the artifacts, they were inspired by the treasure trove to create the Arabia Steamboat Museum and keep the collection together. Thirty years after excavation, the family-run operation is still cleaning and preserving artifacts for display.

Driving through Kansas City, we stopped in a forest park to shake some wild persimmon trees, easily identified by their dark, cubical bark. Four small persimmons fell to the ground; three were still firm and astringent tasting, the fourth mushy and sweet.

Persimmon trees (Diospyros virginiana) have distinctive bark.

Persimmon are highly astringent until fully mushy ripe.

Elixirs remain bottled for use.

243

William Clark established Fort Osage as a trading post in 1808, only two years after the Lewis and Clark Expedition.

Rolling back the wheel of time, we toured Fort Osage National Historic Landmark downriver at Sibley, Missouri. William Clark first noted the bluff overlooking the river in 1804, then passed by again during their 1806 return trip from the Pacific Ocean. In 1808 he led a team back to establish Fort Osage as a trading post.

The U.S. government ran a series of trading posts like Fort Osage to undersell private traders who charged Indians extortive prices and often sold alcohol, inflaming relations on the frontier. The town of Sibley was named after George C. Sibley who ran the profitable operation for the government.

Fort Osage was abandoned in 1822 as the Osage Indians ceded land and migrated west ahead of white settlement. The site was rediscovered by archaeologists in the 1940s and subsequently rebuilt based on the foundations, aided by surveys and drawings produced by William Clark.

Back at Bill Fessler's place, we were joined by Bill Nichols of the Sierra Club, who brought barbecue dinner with him. Bill recently led a group down the Jefferson River Canoe Trail in Montana, one of the three rivers that come together to form the Missouri. Bill provided a detailed breakdown of their experiences and challenges and an estimate of the tourist dollars the group contributed to the Montana economy. From Lewis and Clark to the Steamboat Arabia to new friends around the campfire, we found ourselves connected by the great Missouri River.

Site Administrator Fred Goss managed the gift shop, trade for a new era.

The black rat snake (Pantherophis obsoletus) helps control rodents.

Instant vanilla pudding helped solidify my paw paw pie.

Chinese praying mantis
(Tenodera aridifolia sinensis)

We played Shanleya's Quest by lamplight and enjoyed a warm fire at Bill Fessler's place.

Photo by Scott Robinson

Digging in with a power stroke to launch from shore into the main current.

"Set out after a heavy Shower of rain and proceeded on the Same Course of last night passed a large butifull Prarie on the S. S. opposit a large Island, Calld Saukee Prarie, a gentle breese from the S. W. Some butiful high lands on the L. S. passed Som verry Swift water to day, I saw Pelicans to day on a Sand bar, my servant York nearly loseing an eye by a man throwing Sand into it."

—William Clark, June 20, 1804

We toured the Battle of Lexington State Historic Site.

Taste of Freedom

Lewis and Clark often referred to the crew as "the men" or "a man" without specifying names. Clark didn't elaborate why a member of their expedition threw sand in York's eyes near today's Lexington, Missouri, but it was apparently an intentional act. The Corps of Discovery consisted of white men, many raised in the South within the culture of slavery, who may have tormented York for entertainment or because they resented having an African American on the expedition. Barely a month into the journey, the crew wasn't wholly disciplined, and hadn't yet grown together as a team. Over time, however, York played a role equal or greater than that of the other men. Although slaves were prohibited from using firearms at home, York carried a gun on the expedition and proved to be a successful hunter. He worked side-by-side with the men and joined them in celebrations and dancing. York played a critical role in diplomacy with the tribes, impressing Indians who had never seen a black man before. Lewis and Clark honored York by naming a group of islands after him near Townsend, Montana. And when the co-captains polled the crew regarding a location to build a fort for the winter of 1805, they counted votes from both York and Sacagawea.

Having enjoyed a taste of freedom and equality, York requested release after the expedition, which William Clark denied. The two men had grown up side-by-side as playmates, albeit with one as slave and the other as master. Their post-expedition relationship soured, and after several bitter years, Clark finally caved to York's request.

The issue of slavery divided the United States from the outset, with unresolved issues boiling over into the Civil War of 1861-1865. Lexington, Missouri was the site of one early conflict.

We paddled into Lexington Riverfront Park in our continuing journey of rediscovery. The site was closed due to flooding, but locals drove through six-inch-deep stagnant water for several hundred feet to reach the parking lot and boat ramp. Flood debris provided the aura of disorder, as if entering the aftermath of a minor battle. After setting up camp, Scott and I walked into town to visit the Battle of Lexington State Historic Site. It was evening, but we had the good fortune to arrive when the museum was open for a meeting, and we were allowed to tour the exhibits.

In September of 1861, Colonel James A. Mulligan and 3,500 Union soldiers took the high ground, building fortifications around the Masonic College. A natural spring provided water, but inadequate to meet the needs of all the men and horses.

They were surrounded by Major General Sterling Price and 15,000 soldiers of the Missouri State Guard, who largely waited while hot sun and insufficient water wore down Union forces. On the third day the State Guard used wet hemp bales as mobile breastworks, rolling the bales uphill for protection as they advanced on the northern army's position. Mulligan surrendered, bolstering optimism and support for the Confederate cause.

During the battle, one of Price's regiments fired a cannon that hit a column on the county courthouse, immediately across the street from his own headquarters. Although the

The Missouri State Guard advanced on Union troops using wet bales of hemp as mobile breastworks.

Photo by Scott Robinson

A cannonball hit the county courthouse.

cannonball fell out of the hole, it was later permanently affixed in the column for posterity.

The Union lost the battle, but ultimately won the war. Traumatized veterans from North and South streamed up the Missouri River to form blended communities in the goldfields of the Montana Territory. The former mining town of Sterling, not far from my home in Pony, was likely named after Major General Sterling Price, while nearby Sheridan was named after the Union's General Philip Sheridan. My great grandfather Raymond Thomas Beam followed later, moving from Missouri to Montana in 1906.

While the Union victory forcibly held the United States together, the underlying issues and political divisions remained. A century after the South surrendered, the nation was still clawing inch by inch through desegregation and other civil rights issues. Today's political divide largely follows 150-year-old fault lines. America remains shrouded in the fog of war as deeply entrenched sides hurl scathing insults across social media.

We awoke to a different kind of fog, dense and heavy on the river, delaying our departure until we could perceive trees silhouetted against the opposite bank. In our longest day of the journey, we paddled fifty-five miles to the small town of Miami, Missouri, greatly aided by the swift river current.

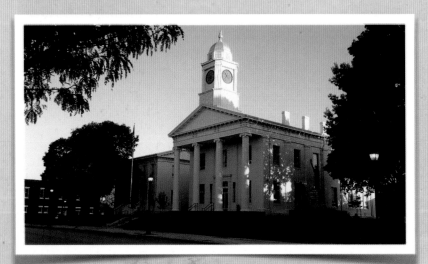

Lafayette County Courthouse, Lexington, Missouri.

A few miles shy of camp we encountered a heavy barge pushing upriver. Conditions were ideal, with calm waters, no wind, and ample room to steer clear of the behemoth watercraft. The initial wake gently rolled across the river in predictable fashion, easily handled by aiming our canoes into the oncoming waves.

A half-mile below the barge, however, we encountered the rear waves. The tow boat pushing the barge dug into the river, creating a massive watery hole followed by a rising, almost fountain-like wave that settled into huge rollers aimed downstream, lifting us several feet on each swell to come crashing back down again.

A mile behind the barge these rear waves merged with side waves echoing off the banks to form turbulence matched only by that of our politically divided country. We heaved up in the air on gridded,

We paddled out into the morning fog. Jubilee eyes trash in the river.

The Highway 13 Ike Skelton Bridge emerges from the fog.

egg-carton-like peaks of nonlinear waves, crashing into pockets that threatened to swamp the canoe at any moment. Two miles behind the barge we were still fighting substantial turbulence. By the time we reached camp, damp and chilled in the last moments of light, the barge was at least five miles upstream, yet the river had not fully regained it's glassy calm.

A change to windy weather necessitated a layover day. River angel Rob Kalthoff generously loaned us his truck to reach nearby Marshall to do laundry, restock supplies, and buy warmer clothes for the chilly weather.

A half-day of paddling then brought us to Glasgow, where we camped in the park and

The fog cleared to reveal a beautiful blue-sky day.

Photo by Scott Robinson

My desk served as a nice sandwich bar for making lunch on the river.

Amanda Haes provided a tour of the Lewis Library.

celebrated Chris's birthday with delicious pizza at Muddy Mo Pizzaria.

I visited the Lewis Library, funded by Benjamin Lewis, who earned his fortune raising hemp and tobacco before the Civil War. A personal friend of Abraham Lincoln, Lewis donated money to the Union and voluntarily freed his slaves, hiring anyone who wanted to stay. In 1864 he was captured and tortured by outlaw rebel Bill Anderson who considered Lewis a traitor to the southern cause.

Lewis miraculously escaped after being severely beaten and trampled by a horse, but died from the injuries two years later, recounted librarian Amanda Haes. Such is the price of liberty and freedom. In his will, Lewis provided funds to build the stately library, which opened in 1867. It has become the oldest library west of the Mississippi to remain in continuous operation.

Benjamin Lewis willed funds to build the library, in operation since 1867.

The sun rises behind a bluff of colorful trees.

Cooler temperatures brought on the fall colors.

"At 8 ms. passed the mouth of a Creek Called Saline or Salt R on the L. Sd. this ⟨Creek⟩ River is about 30 yds. wide, and has So many Licks & Salt Springs on its banks that the Water of the Creek is Brackish, one Verry large Lick is 9 ms. up on the left Side   the water of the Spring in this Lick is Strong as one bushel of the water is said to make 7 lb. of good Salt."

—William Clark, June 6, 1804

A River Relieved

Paddling the channelized Missouri River provided a leaf-by-leaf transition into fall colors, starting with isolated pockets of reds and yellows as far back as Sioux City. The colors gradually increased downriver, then stalled and began rewinding towards summer greens as we raced southward. However, the cold front that overtook us slowed our progress while accelerating the changing colors. Our southern migration halted when the Missouri turned east at Kansas City, allowing fall colors to engulf us from the river banks.

Fall colors here are not like the brilliant carpet of gold I know at home, where uniform forests of cottonwoods turn bright yellow along the rivers. Colors here are more diverse, reflecting the diversity of trees, but also more muted, like the daubed brush strokes of an impressionist painting. A thousand shades of yellow, orange, and red mingle with a background of lingering green, subdued by intermingled grays and browns. Here the cottonwoods seem to drop their leaves without a color phase.

The orange-brown leaves of a sycamore light up the riverbank. Limestone cliffs date back to the Mississippian Period 358.9 to 323.2 mya.

We were told the channelized river would be boring, "every curve the same" for 750 miles. But with the swift current and ever-changing leaves, we enjoyed front row seats to the best show on fall TV. The addition of limestone bluffs made this scrolling painting one of the most scenic parts of the Missouri River.

Downstream from Glasgow, we passed near Boone's Lick State Historic Site, a mile northeast of the river. The lower Missouri was already well known to settlers before William Clark noted the abundance of salt licks. Just one year later, Daniel Boone's sons Nathan and Daniel Morgan Boone partnered with James and Jesse Morrison to commercialize the area's largest salt spring.

Salt production was very labor-intensive prior to industrialization. At Boone's Lick salt works, workers heated brine water in iron kettles to steam off the water, leaving crystallized salt behind. Cooking down 250 to 300 gallons of brine water produced one bushel of salt. The business grew to employ twenty men laboring over sixty kettles. They produced thirty bushels of salt per day, which was shipped downstream to St. Louis via keelboats and sold for $2.50 per bushel.

Evening brought us to Cooper's Landing, a "must-stop" marina and campground on the Missouri River where Churchill Clark carved two dugout canoes from a single cottonwood tree prior to carving Belladonna Beaver in Montana. Normally a lively place, Cooper's Landing was in recovery from earlier flooding and in transition to new ownership. Unusually chilly weather and cancelled music venues kept the crowds away, but site manager Rodney invited us to dine with him for a delicious spread of baked catfish.

We drifted downriver gazing at the many hues of fall colors.

We camped two nights at Cooper's Landing Campground and Marina.

253

Friend Michael Morgan reached out and offered to chauffeur us around nearby Columbia. At the University of Missouri we toured the Museum of Anthropology, which includes the Grayson Archery Exhibit of bows and arrows from around the world. The Museum of Archaeology in the same building took us off-theme to explore Egyptian, Greek, Roman, and other European artifacts and art. Although the museums were small and lacked signage outside the building, the collections were of the highest quality.

Headed back to camp, we enjoyed a short hike to Eagle Bluffs Overlook, exploring trees and shrubs along the way. I saw my first-ever sassafras tree, whose roots were the original source of root beer flavoring. Michael pointed out the unique leaves with three different shapes, a "football, ghost, and glove," as he teaches it to children.

We stopped along the road to check out the base-ball-sized, brainy-looking Osage orange fruits, which smell slightly citrusy. Originally eaten and

Mississippian pottery in the Grayson Archery Exhibit at the Museum of Anthropology, University of Missouri.

Sassafras (Sassafras albidum) has three different leaf shapes.

Osage orange (Maclura pomifera) was originally eaten by megafauna.

Changing weather makes for spectacular sunsets on the Missouri River, here our last night at Cooper's Landing.

Trash imported from Fiji, 7,000 miles away.

distributed by megafauna, such as mastodons and giant ground sloths, the trees have substantially lost territory since the oversized herbivores went extinct after the last Ice Age. Several species of Osage orange went extinct without their co-evolved companions.

Saline seeps and falling leaves are not all that enters the river. A small trail of litter peppers the Missouri all the way from Montana, growing visibly worse below population centers such as Kansas City. I plucked a floating water bottle from the river, imported from Fiji, nearly 7,000 miles away, the non-degradable container now littering this beautiful river. Flood waters exacerbated the trash problem, picking up random goods and trash from every private and public parcel along the way.

A half-day of paddling brought us to Wilson's Serenity Point opposite Jefferson City, the capitol of Missouri. Here we connected with Missouri River Relief, the premier nonprofit organization working to benefit our nation's longest river. MRR offers river ecology classes to students and teachers and hosts three or four major river clean-up days each year. On this day they worked with 200 dedicated volunteers to collect trash from ten miles of riverbank along the east side.

Rain was settling in when we arrived, dispersing most of the volunteers. We joined the remaining crew to sort recyclables from trash. The clean-up gathered 254 bags of trash, plus boatloads of beadboard insulation, 41 tires, a chemical tank, and a whole slew of propane tanks, hot water

Litter is unfortunately abundant along much of the lower Missouri.

Missouri River Relief organized a litter clean-up day near Jefferson City.

Volunteers sorted recyclables from the trash.

heaters, mini-refrigerators, chest freezers, and coolers. Crews found not just one message in a bottle, but ten of them over the ten-mile clean up. The waste more than filled the rented construction dumpster, the excess bags stacked until an additional dumpster arrived.

In the aftermath of flooding, the Missouri Department of Natural Resources reported finding more than 740 chemical containers in the river, varying in size from half-gallon buckets to 500,000-gallon tanks, most thought to have originated on flooded farms in Nebraska and Iowa. The tanks contained chemicals such as ammonia, diesel fuel, pesticides, and other farm chemicals that could poison the river.

Lewis and Clark Monument at the state capitol by sculptor Sabra Tull Meyer features York, Lewis, Seaman, Clark, and George Drouillard.

My impression from nearly five months of paddling is that far more trash enters the river than is readily visible along the banks. There is likely a steady stream of garbage tumbling along the river bottom to the Mississippi and down to the Gulf of Mexico. I visited Padre Island National Seashore in Texas two years ago, awed by the amount of trash heaved onto the beaches from the swirling currents of the Gulf of Mexico. It is estimated that 40 percent of the trash in the Gulf comes from the Missouri - Mississippi watershed.

We unintentionally contributed litter through 2,000 miles of paddling, leaving behind a small trail of missed hats, sunglasses, lids, silverware, and even a fishing pole that disappeared over the side of a canoe. However, we more than offset our footprint by picking up trash, occasionally finding useful gear along the way, such as sunglasses and a fishing net.

Solving the litter problem requires a multi-faceted approach that addresses everything from disposable containers to new setbacks along flood-prone waterways. But that isn't an excuse for individual apathy. There wouldn't be a litter problem if each person simply picked up more garbage than they dropped. It is easy to blame the schmucks who litter. Yet, equally to blame are those who dismiss litter as someone else's responsibility or beneath their dignity to clean up. The world's problems are immense, yet readily manageable if each person contributes to the extent readily within their means.

From Serenity Point I enjoyed a walk across the bridge to visit Lewis and Clark Trailhead Plaza near the capitol building. We camped overnight with the Relief crew, enjoying the warmth of good company around a hardwood fire that dried our damp clothes even during continued sprinkles.

A train snakes along the Missouri River at Jefferson City.

Fall colors light up the riverbanks.

"About 2 oClock P. M we arrived at Saint Charles, where we passed the Evening with a great deal of satisfaction, and chearfulness, and all our men appeared to be in good spirits. We shall waite here for Captain Lewis, who is to meet us from Saint Louis;— Saint Charles is a Village settled by French Inhabitants. It is a handsome situation, laying on the North side of the River contains about 80 Houses, built in the french fashion, and has a small Roman Catholic Chapel."

—Joseph Whitehouse, May 16, 1804

Advance to St. Charles

Belladonna and Jubilee.

"Nice canoe. Did you make that?" Yeah. I carved it last summer with Churchill Clark, a direct descendent of William Clark. "Oh wow, it's really beautiful. What kind of wood is it?" Douglas fir. "Douglas fir? How much does that thing weigh?" At least 500 lbs. I haven't weighed it yet. "It's really beautiful. Where are y'all paddling to?" St. Louis. We started from Three Forks, Montana. "Yeah? Wait. What? You're paddling from where?!?" We're doing the whole Missouri River from Three Forks, Montana to St. Louis. "That's a long way. How long you been on the river?" We left home June first. "June first! That was a while ago... what, like three months?!?" Five months. "Five months?!? Let's see, June, July, August, September, October... oh my, that's a long time... how can y'all afford to take so much time off work?"

A freshwater muscle exercises its one foot.

We've answered variations of the same questions nearly every day of the expedition, that last question usually preceded by a look of confusion and bewilderment—as if we came from another planet where people don't have jobs. For us, the answers are all different, yet united by a common theme. Chris works as a carpenter to save up money, then leaves to go on big adventures. He's taken the last two years off work. Scott worked as a mechanical engineer making medical devices for the past fifteen years. He quit his job to join the expedition, planning a major life transition afterwards.

John, who finished the river ahead of us, does wilderness therapy work with troubled teens. There are few expenses when camping with kids for weeks at a time, so it's easy to save thousands of dollars, then quit and live off the savings.

Photo by Mike Langille (www.thisishermann.com)

Chris and I paddle through challenging and unnerving whirlpools into Hermann, Missouri.

Invasive zebra muscles cling to a rock as floodwaters recede.

Many of my friends have chosen transient lifestyles, hopping from one adventure to another in quests of exploration and enlightenment. Owning a house makes me the anomaly. If I want to dismiss the employment question quickly, I say I'm an author and I'm writing a book about our river trip. People like that answer. It fits cultural expectations that perpetual work is necessary. The actual answer is more complicated, but readily evident in quaint rural towns along the river.

With warm weather growing scarce, we took advantage of a nice day to paddle forty-five miles from Jefferson City to the charming riverside town of Hermann. We pitched our tents in the city park and joined river angels Gary and Marcia Leabman for a cozy evening of homemade pizza and local history.

Hermann is one of many scenic historic towns along the Missouri.

Every day brought more scenes of grandeur with limestone cliffs and fall colors.

Historic towns along the lower Missouri were built on bluffs, taking the high ground for flood protection. Brick houses are common, intermingled with wood frame structures. When Deb gave us a tour at White Cloud, Kansas, she pointed out modest, but solid houses that were selling for $8,000 to $10,000. In Weston, Missouri, Wendy told us how real estate prices were reasonable, but shot up as the town became a tourist destination. Hermann has also been discovered, driving up real estate prices.

Most people buy an expensive home near a job, but houses cost much less where jobs are scarce. It's not difficult to cut expenses long enough to save

Lance Stroheker welcomed us to New Haven. John Colter lived here after his adventures in Montana.

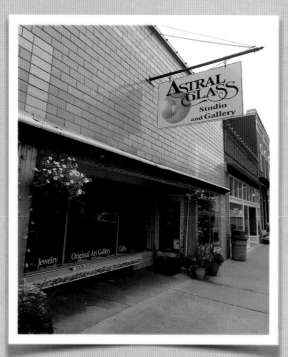

We visited Astral Glass Studio.

Photo by Scott Robinson

Gary and Lance helped us blow glass ornaments.

money and pay cash, typically $20,000 to $50,000, for a modest house in urban and rural communities throughout the United States.

In the lifelong game of Monopoly, people tend to invest beyond their means, starting out with properties like Marvin Gardens, Pennsylvania Avenue, or Boardwalk, which are too expensive to develop. My favorites were always the violet-purple properties of Virginia Avenue, States Avenue, and St. Charles Place, where houses and hotels were affordable, yet brought a decent return on the investment.

Passing by New Haven, we stopped to visit Lance Stroheker and Gary Rice at Astral Glass Studio. Gary moved the business there after being priced out of California. A few years ago Lance and Gary paddled the upper half of the Missouri River. Now they invite fellow thru-paddlers to make glass-blown Christmas ornaments and sign their wall. Lance

Gary and Lance attach a loop to Scott's ornament.

bought several acres of inexpensive land nearby, and he is preparing to build his own home.

That's how I started out in the early 1990s. My then-partner and I worked part-time in wilderness therapy, then bought land, lived in a tent, and paid cash for building materials. Our combined income was only $10,000 to $12,000, but we gained $50,000 in annual value through property improvements and avoided mortgage interest. Living debt free with few monthly expenses, there was no need for a 9-to-5 job, providing ample time to pursue a writing career, raise a family, and go on great adventures.

Down the street from Astral Glass, Shane Camden is fulfilling his entrepreneurial dream in a warehouse he bought from the city for $1 and his pledge to renovate the structure. He launched Paddle Stop New Haven, where he produces beautiful hand-crafted wooden canoes, kayaks, and stand-up-paddle boards.

Scott and his partner Margie have "telescoped down" from mortgaged houses to renting and will transition to a van after the expedition, giving up cubicle life for a life of adventure, supplemented by part-time work to pay minimal bills while incubating their own entrepreneurial ideas. Scott has done it before, landing on Free Parking every time around the board. It's a great way to save money quickly to invest in adventures or assets. A monthly gym membership provides a convenient place for showers and exercise.

Paddling to Washington, Missouri we found another booming tourist town where river angels Bruce and Marvis Templar and their friend Ron treated us out to dinner, eager to hear our stories from the trail. Then we finally advanced to St. Charles, a short twenty-eight miles from the confluence where the Missouri River joins the Mississippi. Here our triumphant race to the finish line was waylaid by another major storm.

Fresh beaver work along the river.

Missouri / October 29 / Washington to St. Charles

For the original Corps of Discovery, St. Charles was the last town of substance before heading upriver. William Clark measured the Missouri River there and calculated it to be 720 yards wide.

The expedition camped for five nights while awaiting Lewis's arrival from nearby St. Louis. We camped for three nights while the storm dropped heavy rain that gradually tapered off to drifting snowflakes.

The Lewis and Clark Boat House and Museum kindly let us pitch our tents in the sheltered, open-walled lower level of the building where they keep a replica keelboat and two pirogues. While Lewis and Clark were on the cusp of starting their great adventure, we were equally close to finishing ours.

I am immensely grateful to Scott as navigator and co-leader.

Approaching Veterans Memorial Bridge at St. Charles, Missouri.

Bridges grow taller closer to the Mississippi.

"We left our establishment at the mouth of the river du Bois or Wood river, a small river which falls into the Mississippi, on the east-side, a mile below the Missouri, and having crossed the Mississippi proceeded up the Missouri on our intended voyage of discovery... The day was showery and in the evening we encamped on the north bank six miles up the river. Here we had leisure to reflect on our situation, and the nature of our engagements: and, as we had all entered this service as volunteers, to consider how far we stood pledged for the success of an expedition, which the government had projected; and which had been undertaken for the benefit and at the expence of the Union: of course of much interest and high expectation."

—Patrick Gass, May 14, 1804

Gateway

The Lewis and Clark Expedition started a year before it began. In Philadelphia, Meriwether Lewis immersed in crash courses for medicine, botany, zoology, and surveying, plus he learned how to make celestial observations necessary to determine latitude and longitude. He oversaw construction of the keelboat and engaged in the biggest shopping trip in then-American history. Lewis and Clark independently recruited men for the expedition and migrated slowly westward. However, they were not allowed to cross west of the Mississippi, since the Louisiana Purchase had not yet transferred from Spain to France to the United States. The expedition wintered over at the starting gate, building a small fort named Camp Dubois on the Wood River in today's Illinois before officially launching the Corps of Discovery on May 14, 1804.

While they sat at the starting line, our Missouri River Corps of Rediscovery stalled near the finish line, camping for three days in St. Charles waiting out a storm. We took the opportunity to tour Cahokia Mounds State Historic Site on the east side of the Mississippi in Illinois with my friend Larry Kinsella.

The Boat House Museum allowed us to camp in the gated open-air lower level.

Artist rendering of Cahokia Mounds in their prime.

Larry Kinsella treated us to a great tour of the historic site.

The Birdman was an important symbol to Cahokian people.

Cahokia is the largest pre-Columbia archaeological site north of Mexico. The city covered six square miles, including about 120 earthen mounds constructed to different sizes and shapes. The mounds were solid, used as platforms for ceremonial houses, burials, sacrifices, and home sites for city leaders.

Building all the earthen mounds required an estimated 55 million cubic feet of soil, mostly hauled in woven pack baskets by thousands of laborers over many decades. The largest mound rises 100 feet high. The base is similar in size to the Great Pyramid of Giza. At its peak around 1100 A.D., Cahokia was home to up to 20,000 people, bigger than London at the time.

Cahokia fits a common theme among horticultural peoples worldwide. Surplus food led to population booms and idle citizenry. Building mounds, temples, and pyramids for purported religious purposes was an effective jobs creation program to keep people occupied, thus maintaining social order.

Our civilization is not so different. We portaged around several great earthen mounds as dams on the Missouri River. Interpretive displays at the corresponding visitor centers touted the benefits of building the dams, including flood control, irrigation, hydro-electricity, and "to create jobs," the raison d'etre always tacked onto the end of the list. Thousands of workers were employed building the dams, one of our society's means of keeping people occupied to maintain social order.

Cahokia declined for unknown reasons around the year 1300 and was abandoned by 1350. William Clark visited the northern edge of the city on January 9, 1804, where he noted an Indian fortress consisting of nine short mounds in a circle and *"great quantities of Earthen ware & flints."*

Larry Kinsella has volunteered at Cahokia Mounds for forty years, working on archaeological digs, reconstruction projects, and interpretive displays. He made a number of the stone axes and knives featured in interpretive displays, which is how I met him, through our mutual background teaching Stone Age living skills.

We also toured Mastodon State Historic Site south of St. Louis. While mammoths lived in grassland steppe habitat near glaciers, mastodons lived in forests farther south and ate woody browse, giving rise to very different types of teeth. Larry helped excavate a

Dioramas depict daily life for people of Cahokia Mounds.

Stone axes were used to cut trees for houses and fortifications.

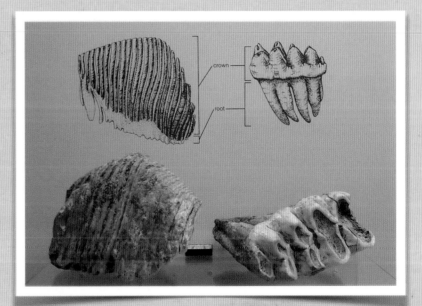

A mammoth tooth (left) differs greatly from a mastodon tooth (right).
Mastodon State Historic Site / Missouri State Parks

We met up with paddler Mark Fingerhut (back right) for dinner.

Jubilee was dog-napped twice in St. Charles.

Families walk the streets of historic St. Charles to trick-or-treat on Halloween.

mastodon tusk on display and he made a series of spear points to illustrate the flintknapping process used by Ice Age hunters.

Scott's girlfriend Margie flew in from Colorado and joined us for dinner with Mark Fingerhut. Mark paddled the Missouri River this year, starting upstream where the Madison River exits Yellowstone National Park. He paddled by Three Forks, Montana two weeks ahead of our launch, so we were behind him all the way.

Bedded down in our tents below the Boat House Museum, people passing by wouldn't have known we were there. However, someone encountered an overly friendly puppy and dog-napped Jubilee as a lost dog. Chris spent the following day at a coffee shop searching online lost pet notices and fortunately got her back. She was dog-napped again a day later, only minutes after being released to run off her pent-up puppy energy. Chris paid $35 to retrieve her from the pound, following up with a dog tag and phone number on her collar.

Margie joined us as we paddled out of St. Charles, doing an easy 25-mile day to Columbia Bottom, only 3.5 miles from the end of the Missouri River where it joins the Mississippi.

Margie joined us for a day on the water.

We offered tobacco to the river.

We offered tobacco to the big rivers on behalf of the Turtle Mountain Chippewa of North Dakota, whom we met at their community pow wow at Trenton Lake in early August. Brett and Anita Williamson sent the tobacco pouch with us containing the community's prayers for the river and our journey. We added our prayers for special people we met along the way, and gave a final thank you to the river at our last camp of the journey.

Our final day of paddling was largely symbolic. We awoke to heavy frost, a sure sign to wrap up the trip. We paddled out into the chilly morning, soon reaching the confluence where the Missouri joins the Mississippi. There wasn't any significant turbulence where the waters merged, just two great rivers flowing together like a slow-moving lake.

Our final sunset on the Missouri River featured an orange-blue hue.

Gateway Arch on the Mississippi River is the symbolic end point for Missouri River paddlers.

The original Corps of Discovery continued fifteen miles down the Mississippi to end their 28-month expedition at St. Louis on September 23, 1806, where William Clark reported, *"We Suffered the party to fire off their pieces as a Salute to the Town. we were met by all the village and received a harty welcom from it's inhabitants."*

We followed their lead, paddling to the Gateway Arch, the iconic symbol of St. Louis. Conceived in the 1940s and completed in 1965, the 630-foot-tall stainless steel arch was created as a *"memorial to the men who made possible the western territorial expansion of the United States, particularly President Jefferson, his aides Livingston and Monroe, the great explorers, Lewis and Clark, and the hardy hunters, trappers, frontiersmen and pioneers who contributed to the territorial expansion and development of these United States."* In today's more politically correct terms, that would make it a monument to colonialism and the subjugation of Native American peoples.

That's the great challenge in celebrating American history. Thomas Jefferson and William Clark both owned slaves, and Meriwether Lewis supervised slaves on his mother's plantation. All three men helped bring about the subjugation of Native Americans, especially William, who continued the work of his elder brother George Rogers Clark to remove Indians from all lands east of the Mississippi. We cannot and should not bury our history, but we can own and re-interpret it.

I grew up with Montana history where General George Custer was slaughtered by wild Indians at the Custer Battlefield National Monument, otherwise known as "Custer's Last Stand." In a re-appraisal of our history, Congress renamed the site as the Little Bighorn Battlefield National Monument in 1991. The revamped park includes a memorial to the Indians who fought and died there, as well as a telling of their side of the story. Piccc by piece we are telling a more authentic narrative of our history, and that is an achievement to be appreciated and honored.

In St. Louis, the Jefferson National Expansion Memorial was renamed Gateway Arch National Park in 2018. We planned our arrival for Sunday,

St. Louis as seen from the top of Gateway Arch.

Our last morning on the water was frosty cold. Jubilee wore a cape.

The three of us, Chris, Tom, and Scott, completed the journey together.

the least busy day to mingle with the big ships in the Port of St. Louis. First we paddled over the notorious "chain of rocks," submerged so deeply below flood waters that the river flowed over the obstacle as a smooth wave.

Shortly thereafter, we were joined by Mike Clark of Big Muddy Adventures (unrelated to William Clark) for the final gauntlet through the port. Headwinds kicked up turbulence, aggravated by passing barges, but manageable overall. We paddled to the Arch, tied off the canoes, and ascended the stairs with our arms and paddles outstretched in victory at the conclusion of our five-month descent of the Missouri River!

That was the fantasy anyway. Waves threatened to batter the canoes against the flooded stairway, forcing us to abort the landing. We paddled another quarter-mile downriver to a boat ramp, while our greeting party and Channel 4 News crew raced to their cars to catch up. We completed our journey on November 3rd, five months and three days after we launched from Three Forks, Montana. John Gentry, also from our group, completed his journey two weeks earlier, having paddled ahead from Nebraska.

Many people are under the illusion that we worked hard and suffered greatly on our expedition. I would describe the experience as akin to turtles drifting down the river on a log. John, Chris, and I all had extensive outdoor experience. Scott likely gained the most during the journey, transitioning from an office cubicle to canoe to a new life of adventure. For all of us, it was a great privilege to paddle through the heart of America, see beautiful scenery, study our history, and meet some of the nicest people on the planet.

With little fanfare, we loaded the canoes and bid hasty goodbyes. Scott and Margie rushed home to Colorado while Chris, Jubilee, and I enjoyed Mike Clark's hospitality for two days while awaiting a ride back north.

The Missouri River Corps of Rediscovery joined a surprisingly short list of all known Missouri River expeditions since 1962, maintained as a database by Norman Miller of Livingston, Montana at www.MissouriRiverPaddlers.com.
Thank you for reading along and being part of this journey!

Chris and I and Mike Clark toured William Clark's grave at Bellefontaine Cemetery in St. Louis, the final stop of our journey.

The End

About the Author

"Life is too short for ordinary dreams," says author, educator, and conservationist Thomas J. Elpel. The loss of his father at an early age instilled in Tom an ever-present sense of the ticking clock and the need to live one's dreams before time runs out.

At the age of sixteen, he signed up for a 26-day walkabout with Boulder Outdoor Survival School, learning basic wilderness survival skills while hiking 250 miles through the desert canyons of southern Utah. That led to a 500-mile walk across Montana two years out of high school.

Tom has not worked a 9 to 5 job, but did short stints in carpentry and wilderness therapy, leading troubled teens on expeditions in Utah, Arizona, and Idaho. He spent a winter brain-tanning hides for sale as his first attempt at self-employment.

He built his passive solar stone and log dream home and went on to establish a successful writing career and publishing company, HOPS Press, LLC. Tom is the founder of Green University®, LLC, providing wilderness skills classes for adults, as well as Outdoor Wilderness Living School, LLC (OWLS) through which he provides immersive nature connection experiences for public school kids. He is president of the Jefferson River Chapter of the Lewis and Clark Trail Heritage Foundation and founder of the Jefferson River Canoe Trail.

Along the way, Tom raised a family and took his children on many great adventures, including two weeks paddling Montana's Upper Missouri Wild and Scenic River. With his kids now grown and out of the nest, and forty years after the loss of his own father, Tom sought to paddle the entire Missouri River as his next great adventure.

Photo by Dirk Rohrbach

Tom Elpel with Belladonna Beaver at Fort Benton, Montana.

"I love this game!! I've played it dozens of times now and each time I teach someone to play it they walk away and return later and tell me all about how they can't stop thinking about how everything else in nature works. They're all becoming naturalists just by playing a game."

—Chris Hyde,
Natureversity

Wildlife Web
Dynamic ecology strategy game
Created by Thomas J. Elpel

*Adventure, luck, and cunning provide
hours of fun for family and friends!*

Can you forage or hunt for food, find a mate, and raise your young... without becoming someone else's lunch? Welcome to *Wildlife Web*, a game where you participate in the web of life.

Wildlife Web is an exciting, dynamic game of strategy where adventure, luck, and cunning provide hours of fun for family and friends, recommended for ages 9 to 99.

Do you want to be a mountain lion, deer, or elk? This surprisingly realistic game enables players to experience life as any of 50 different animals, and each animal has a mate.

How do you strategize to eat, mate, stay alive, and pass your genes along to the next generation? Each animal has a special survival rating, plus unique abilities to help when hunting or defending against predators.

Wildlife Web is competitive and cooperative. On the one hand, the game features classic predator-prey relationships where mountain lions hunt rabbits, deer, elk, or bison with the roll of the dice.

On the other hand there is cooperation as robins warn the deer as a mountain lion approaches. Your deer gains 2 extra defense points for every robin on the table. Try it out... can you navigate the web of life?

See all books, games, and videos at www.HOPSPress.com.

"I own both Shanleya's Quest and Botany in a Day and I can't say enough great things about them. I teach mostly 3rd to 8th graders, and my goal is primarily to help my students establish a relationship with plants. Your materials are incredibly supportive of that, not to mention engaging, effective and fun."

—Katharine K.

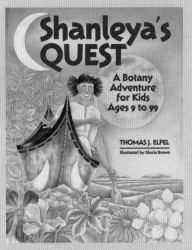

Shanleya's Quest is available in English and Spanish.

Shanleya's Quest
A Botany Adventure for Kids Ages 9 to 99
By Thomas J. Elpel, author of *Botany in a Day*

In a mythical world where time is a liquid that falls as rain, Shanleya paddles her canoe out to the "Tree Islands" to learn the plant traditions of her people. The evolutionary tree of life becomes a literal part of the story, buried up to its branch-tips (the "islands") in an ocean of Time that just keeps getting deeper and deeper. Each island home to a separate family of plants and an unforgettable Guardian with lessons to teach about the identification and uses of those plants.

Readers young and old can join *Shanleya's Quest*, learning the patterns to correctly identify more than 45,000 species of plants to their proper families. *Shanleya's Quest* will change the way you see the natural world, enabling you to experience nature in a new and magical way that you probably never imagined possible.

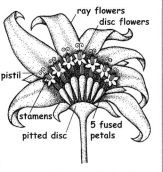

Aster Family
composite flowers

ray flowers
disc flowers
pistil
stamens
5 fused petals
pitted disc

Asters have "composite" flowerheads with multiple small flowers attached to a pitted disc.

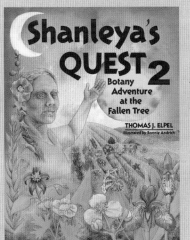

Shanleya's Quest 2
Botany Adventure at the Fallen Tree

Adelia, Katyln, and Peter embark on a magical journey back in time to meet the legendary botanist. Together they explore the world that bloomed after the fall of the Great Tree. They examine old flower fossils, discover new plant families and their guardians, and experience the wonderful world of plants. Readers young will learn essential patterns for identifying 30,000 plants to the correct families, plus the story includes an overview of the edible and medicinal properties of those plant families.

Read the books.
Play the card games:

- *Memory*
- *Slap Flower*
- *Crazy Flowers*
- *Wildflower Rummy*
- *Shanleya's Harvest*

(Games sold separately.)

Go to www.HOPSPress.com to order!

The adventure continues!

Looking for life-changing resources?
Check out these additional books by Thomas J. Elpel:

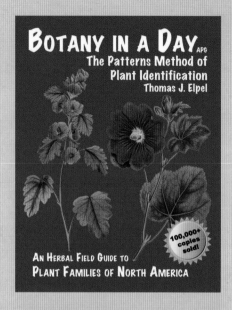

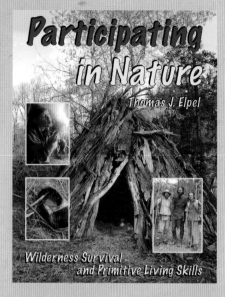

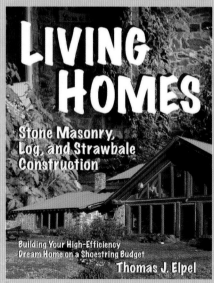

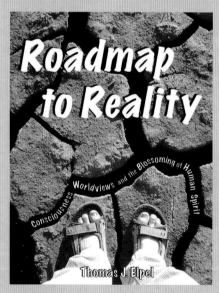

Go to www.HOPSPress.com to order!